David Bonamy

Technical English 2
SECOND EDITION

Course Book and eBook

Contents

Unit / Section		Function / Skill	Grammar / Discourse	Lexis / Technology
Unit 1 Action	1.1 Teamwork p.4	Describing a series of actions Giving a series of instructions	Revision of present simple and imperative	Maintenance: *adjust, lower, raise, tighten* … Equipment: *flap, hose, jack, nozzle* …
	1.2 Training p.6	Reporting jobs in progress Reporting jobs completed	Revision of present continuous and present perfect Word order of phrasal verb: *take off the tyres/take them off*	Phrasal verbs: *pump in, switch off* …
	1.3 Method p.8	Discussing how things work Describing method	Method: *by* + gerund Method: *by/using; by using/by means of* + noun	Activation devices: *cord, lever, screen, sensor* …
Unit 2 Work	2.1 Routines p.10	Describing routines Explaining future plans Job descriptions	Use of present simple: job descriptions and routines Use of present continuous: current actions and future plans	Line management: *report to, supervise* … Job titles: *Assistant, Crew, Operator, Supervisor*
	2.2 Plans p.12	Stating plans and intentions Arranging a meeting by phone Writing emails	Future: present continuous; *going to* Intentions: */plan/want/intend/hope* + *to* Formulae in emails	Work tasks: *hold (a meeting), inspect, meet, run (a fire drill)*
	2.3 New job p.14	Talking about your CV Job adverts and interviews	Revision of past simple	Headings on a CV: *experience, qualification, training* … Syllable stress: *engineer, engine, engineering*
Review Unit A p.16				
Unit 3 Comparison	3.1 Limits p.20	Explaining dimension limits Comparing two items	Revision of dimension: *It's 5 m wide/It has a width of; 2 by 3 metres* Comparative adjectives; *too; enough*	Specifications: *diameter, height, length* …
	3.2 Products p.22	Asking, offering and checking Specifying requirements	Modals and contractions: *could, would, shall, I'd* Gerund: *would you mind … ing?* Pronouns *one/ones: Which one? The red one with the cover.*	Customer service: *cancel, catalogue, order* …
	3.3 Equipment p.24	Comparing three or more items Collaborative problem solving Reporting on a meeting	Superlative adjectives: *the -est of; the most/least* (adj) *of*	Engine descriptions: *cheap, expensive, noisy* …
Unit 4 Processes	4.1 Infrastructure p.26	Describing a process	Present simple passive: formation and use Passive with/without *by* + agent	Stages in a process: *casting, cooling, cutting* … Mechanical: *chute, conveyor belt, cylinder* …
	4.2 Manufacturing p.28	Expressing purpose Describing two parallel processes	Purpose clause: *to* + verb Passive + *to*: *The car body is painted to protect it from rust.*	Car assembly: *axle, body, chassis* … Sequence: *finally, first, next* … Simultaneity: *meanwhile, simultaneously*
	4.3 Communications p.30	Describing a process	Relative clauses (non-defining): *which, who*	Telecoms: *dish, frequency, satellite* … Synonyms: *convert/change, receive/get* … Hyphens: *high-frequency, 13-amp* …
Review Unit B p.32				
Unit 5 Descriptions	5.1 Uses p.36	Describing use or function	Gerund: *(used) for* + verb + *-ing* Infinitive: *(designed) to* + infinitive *Act as* + noun: *it acts as a propeller*	Agent nouns in *-er/-or: stabiliser, transmitter, conductor, generator* …
	5.2 Appearance p.38	Describing shape and appearance	*It looks like a dome.* *It is shaped like a dome/dome-shaped.* *It is in the shape of an L/L-shaped.*	Shapes and syllable stress: *cylinder/cylindrical* … Letter shapes: *A-frame, E-clip, U-bend* …
	5.3 Definitions p.40	Giving a definition	Defining relative clauses: *who, which, that* Definition: *A solar panel is a device that converts sunlight into electricity.*	'Type' nouns: *device, instrument, system* …
Unit 6 Procedures	6.1 Safety p.42	Describing safety hazards Explaining safety procedures Expressing necessity	Modals: *must/should/have to/need to* Modal + passive: *helmets must be worn/have to be worn/should be worn*	Warehouse: *aisle, fork, pallet, ramp* … Warning labels: *fragile, keep frozen, keep upright* …
	6.2 Emergency p.44	Brainstorming Recommending action	Revision of zero conditional Necessity: *must/have to/need to* Recommendation: *should*	Scuba diving: *buoy, buoyant, surface* … Rescue/first aid: *artificial respiration, casualty, treatment* …
	6.3 Directions p.46	Giving directions to a location Following directions	Revision of (a) *there is/are*; (b) *if*; (c) *will*; (d) present continuous	Landmarks: *gantry, roundabout, slip road* … Direction phrases: *turn left, straight ahead* …
Review Unit C p.48				

Unit / Section		Function / Skill	Grammar / Discourse	Lexis / Technology
Unit 7 Services	7.1 Technical support p.52	Diagnosing causes Suggesting solutions Certainty and possibility	Certainty/possibility: *must/may/might + be/present continuous/present perfect: I must have done it.* *Try doing …; Why don't you …? You could ….*	Computers: *access, click on, connect, log into …*
	7.2 Reporting to clients p.54	Reporting on work done	Past simple passive: *CCTV cameras were installed on all floors.* Revision: expressing purpose	Buildings: *beam, fire-resistant, structural …*
	7.3 Dealing with complaints p.56	Responding to complaints Sympathising, apologising Reporting damage/faults	Formulae in letters: *I am/was sorry to hear that …/ I am pleased to inform you that … , I look forward to -ing*	Damage: *burnt, crushed, twisted …* Compensation: *refund, replacement …*
Unit 8 Energy	8.1 Wave power p.58	Describing motion Describing how it works Presenting information orally	Revision of a range of language forms	Movement: *clockwise, linear, oscillating, reciprocating, rotary*
	8.2 Engines p.60	Actions in sequence Simultaneous actions A mechanical cycle	Time clauses: *when; as* Adverbials: *after this; at the same time* Cohesion: *this/which* referring to a whole clause	Engine parts: *cam, camshaft, exhaust valve …*
	8.3 Cooling and heating p.62	Describing a flow cycle	Revision of a range of forms	Verb/agent noun/concept noun families: *compress/compression/compressor* Refrigeration: *coil, evaporator, valve …*

Review Unit D p.64

Unit / Section		Function / Skill	Grammar / Discourse	Lexis / Technology
Unit 9 Measurement	9.1 Sports data p.68	Fractions and percentages Expressing approximation Using maintenance schedules	Noun clause: *check/make sure that …* Frequency: *every 3000 km/at 3000-km intervals; whichever is the sooner*	Approximation: *just under/over …* Instruments: *altimeter, barometer …*
	9.2 Sensors p.70	Explaining forces Describing sensors	Noun modifiers: *vehicle crash test dummy*	Forces: *compression, shear, tension …*
	9.3 Positioning p.72	Expressing calculations Expressing measurements	Discourse: *for example, in other words, in addition, however* Indirect *Wh-* question: *find out how deep it is*	Measurement: *altitude, depth, location …* Operators: *equals, multiply by, times …*
Unit 10 Forces	10.1 Properties p.74	Stating objectives Describing properties of materials	Indirect *Yes/No* question: *if/whether* *The aim/objective of the test is to find out if the plastic bends.*	Property nouns: *plasticity, rigidity …* Property adjectives: *plastic, rigid …*
	10.2 Resistance p.76	Resistance to forces Marking stages of a presentation	Modal + passive: *It can't be stretched.* Formulae: *I'd like to begin by/that brings me to/as you can see …*	Property suffixes: *-able/-ible, -proof, -resistant …* Construction: *beam, brace, column …*
	10.3 Results p.78	Explaining results	Result markers: *(and) so, as, because, since, (and) as a result, (and) therefore*	Electrical: *earthed, live, neutral, shock …* Causative verbs: *loosen, strengthen, widen …*

Review Unit E p.80

Unit / Section		Function / Skill	Grammar / Discourse	Lexis / Technology
Unit 11 Design	11.1 Working robots p.84	Explaining strengths/ weaknesses Making suggestions	Noun clause: *the main strength of … is that it can …; I suggest that …*	Robotics: *joystick, robot, voice-activated …* Construction: *girder, scaffolding …*
	11.2 Eco-friendly planes p.86	Using a design brief Giving a presentation	Revision of a range of forms	Aeronautics: *drag, lift, thrust …* Plane parts: *fuselage, wingtip …*
	11.3 Traction kites p.88	Marking stages of a presentation	Formulae and questions: *I'd like to start by asking a question: Why do we need a traction kite?*	Marine: *cargo, mast, sail, supertanker …*
Unit 12 Innovation	12.1 Zero emission p.90	Explaining needs, problems and solutions	Revision of a range of forms Reduced relative clause: *the energy (which is) released during braking*	Environmental: *emission, fossil fuel, greenhouse gas …* Automotive: *acceleration, braking, cruising …* Electrical: *anode, capacitor, cathode …*
	12.2 Technological change p.92	Describing historical processes Describing contemporary processes	Revision of past simple passive Revision of present simple passive	Simple machines: *belt and pulley, rack and pinion …* Oil drilling: *drill bit, drill string, derrick …* Lasers: *lens, fibre-optics …*
	12.3 Vehicle safety p.94	Describing someone's career Conducting an interview	Revision of a range of forms	Car safety systems: *cruise control, impact protection …*

Review Unit F p.96

Grammar summary p.100

Reference section p.108

Extra material p.111

Speed search p.118

Audio script p.120

1 Action

1 Teamwork

START HERE   **1**   **Discuss these questions with a partner.**

- How many mechanics work in a pit-stop crew in a big race?
  a) about 4   b) about 10   c) about 20
- What jobs do they do? List the most important jobs.

READING   **2**   Read this interview with the head of a pit-stop crew. Check your answers to 1.

Making every millisecond count

How do mechanics service a car so quickly in the middle of a car race? Will Peters is chief mechanic and leader of a pit-stop crew. Here he explains his work.

I'm the crew leader, and I have about 20 mechanics in my crew. It's dangerous work, so we wear fire suits and safety helmets. I have four teams changing the wheels: *wheel-gun*, *wheel-on*, *wheel-off* and *wheel-jack*. A fifth team does all the other tasks, such as holding the car steady, cleaning the driver's visor and adjusting the wings of the car.

Every millisecond is important in the middle of a race, so everyone moves quickly and works together as a team. We can finish the job in under three seconds, but we always try to finish it in fewer than two seconds if we can!

00:30.00	About 30 seconds before we start the job, I give the order: 'Get ready!' The four *wheel-on* mechanics bring out the new wheels. The team leader adjusts the air pressure in the tyres.
00:10.00	With about ten seconds to go, the car enters the pit-stop lane and slows down.
00:03.00	Three seconds to go! The car approaches the garage. The teams run into position. I signal to the driver: STOP. The driver slows down and drives towards the crew. The *wheel-gun* team leader signals where to stop and the driver stops the car with the front wheels next to the front wheel guns. A red light switches on in front of the driver. Now all the teams spring into action! GO!

00:00.00	The two wheel-jack team members move forward and place the jacks under the front and rear of the car. They raise the car off the ground and wait in position.
00:00.30	The four wheel-gun mechanics move forward. They loosen the nuts with their wheel guns. Then they move back quickly.
00:00.60	The four wheel-off mechanics move forward. They take the old wheels off and carry them away quickly. Two other mechanics stand at the side and hold the car steady while the other mechanics are changing the wheels.
00:00.90	Now the four wheel-on guys move forward. They put the new wheels on the car and move back quickly. At the side of the car, another mechanic puts his arm into the cockpit and cleans the driver's visor.
00:01.20	The wheel-gun guys move forward and tighten the wheel nuts. Then they step back and press a button on their guns to signal that everything is OK.
00:01.50	The wheel-jack people lower the car to the ground. The front guy swings the handle of the jack to the side away from the car. Then they both take the jacks away quickly and press a button on their jacks to signal that all is OK.
00:02.20	When all the wheel-gun and wheel-jack mechanics have pressed their buttons, the red light in front of the driver changes to green. This signals GO to the driver, but a safety mechanic can stop this and keep the light on red if necessary. As crew leader, I watch the whole process and I can also keep the red light on until it is safe.
00:02.30	When the light changes to green, the car speeds up and leaves the pit-stop lane. It's in the race again.

3 Label the parts.

visor   front   jack   wheel nut
rear   wheel gun   helmet

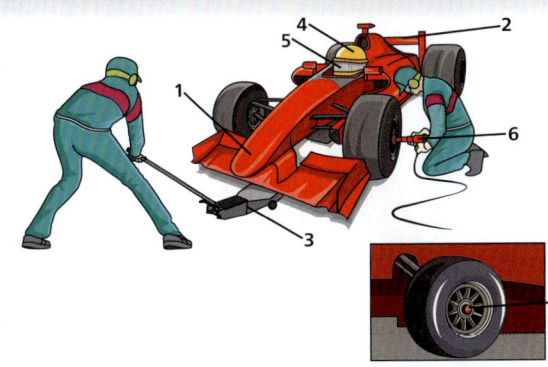

4 Complete this checklist of instructions for each team.

TEAM 1: WHEEL-JACK
1 Place the jacks under the front and rear.
2 Raise _____.
3 WAIT
4 _____.
5 Take _____.

TEAM 2: WHEEL-GUN
1 Loosen the wheel nuts on the old wheels.
2 WAIT.
3 Tighten _____.
4 Press the _____.

TEAM 3: WHEEL-OFF
1 Take the old wheels off.
2 _____.

TEAM 4: WHEEL-ON
1 Bring out the new wheels.
2 Adjust _____.
3 WAIT.
4 Put _____.

TEAM 5: OTHER TASKS
1 Hold the car _____.
2 Clean _____.
3 Adjust _____.

2 Training

START HERE » 1 🔊 1.1 You are a trainee pit-stop mechanic. A trainer is giving you instructions. Listen and write numbers 1–10 to show the correct order of instructions.

Tighten the wheel nuts.		Adjust the air pressure in the tyre.	
Raise the car with the jack.		Bring the new wheel out.	
Loosen the wheel nuts.		Put the new wheel on.	
Take the old wheel off.		Put the jack under the car.	
Take the old wheel away.		Lower the car and take the jack away.	

VOCABULARY » 2 Match the pictures with the verbs in the box.

lift up   pick up   pull out   push in   put down   put on   take away   take off

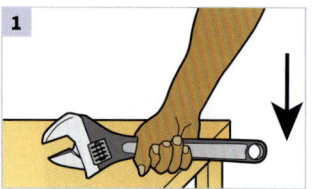   

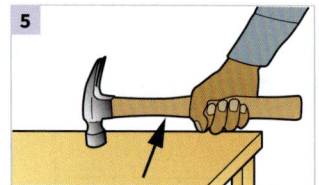 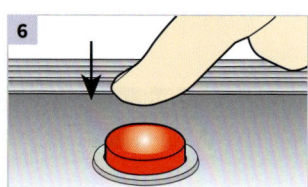 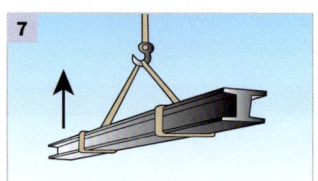 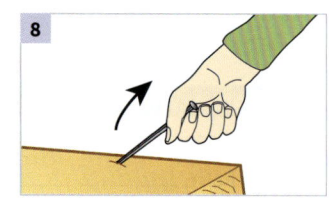

LANGUAGE »

Imperative	Present continuous	Present perfect
Take the tyres off.	I'm taking the tyres off now.	I've taken the tyres off.
Take off the tyres.	I'm taking off the tyres now.	I've taken off the tyres.
Take them off.	I'm taking them off.	I've taken them off.
Not: ~~Take off them.~~	Not: ~~I'm taking off them.~~	Not: ~~I've taken off them.~~

3 🔊 1.2 Listen and respond to these instructions quickly. Confirm (a) what you are doing and then (b) what you have done.

Example: *1 (You hear) Bring out the new tyres. (You say) Right. I'm bringing them out now. OK, I've brought them out.*

SPEAKING » 4 Work in pairs. Make dialogues between a supervisor (S) and a trainee (T) from the checklists.

1	• put new tyres on	done	4	• switch off electricity	done
	• tighten wheel nuts	in progress		• test all circuits	in progress
	• adjust air pressure	not yet done		• find any faults	not yet done
2	• take cover off	done	5	• strip off old paint	done
	• repair computer	in progress		• plaster holes in wall	in progress
	• take out damaged chip	not yet done		• buy new paint	not yet done
3	• replace burnt wire	done	6	• take apart telephone	done
	• switch on power	in progress		• put it together again	in progress
	• check other wires	not yet done		• test it	not yet done

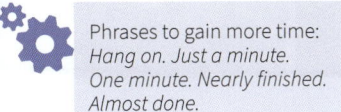

Phrases to gain more time:
Hang on. Just a minute.
One minute. Nearly finished.
Almost done.

S: How are you getting on?
T: I've put the new tyres on. I'm still tightening the wheel nuts. It's almost done.
S: OK, good. Have you adjusted the air pressure yet?
T: No, I haven't done that yet. I'll do it next.

LANGUAGE » *yet* is used with present perfect questions and negatives to emphasise the period of time up to now.

Has Bill finished that job yet? The speaker wanted or expected Bill to finish the job before now. *John hasn't cleaned the car yet.* The speaker wanted or expected John to clean the car before now.

TASK » 5 Work in small groups. Choose one of these car jobs. With your group, make a set of instructions for doing the job.

Changing a wheel

Cleaning a spark plug

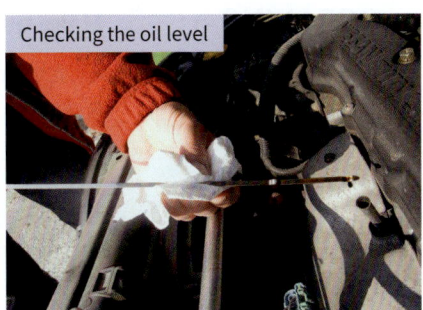
Checking the oil level

6 Turn to page 111. Find useful instructions from the list. Revise your own set of instructions. Rewrite them if necessary, and make them short and simple.

7 Roleplay this situation with someone from another group with a different job.

Student A: You're the manager of a garage. You're showing a new trainee how to do the job. Tell the trainee how to do the job, but don't look at your set of instructions. Give instructions, and check how the trainee is getting on.

First of all, loosen the wheel nuts. Have you done that yet? Good. Right. Now lift up the car with the jack. OK? Well done.

Student B: You're a new trainee in the garage. Follow the manager's instructions. Mime the actions if you can. Tell the manager how you're getting on.

Hang on. Just a minute. No, not yet. I'm still loosening the wheel nuts. It's almost done. OK, I've finished. I've taken it off. What do I do next?

3 Method

START HERE »

1 How do you start or activate these devices?

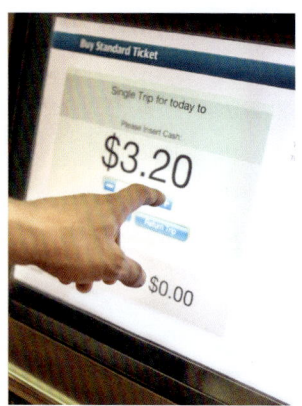    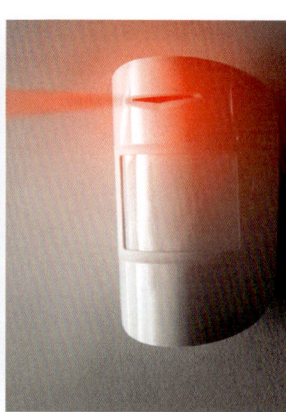

READING »

2 Complete the sentences.

> break   kick   pick up   press   pull   switch on   touch

1 The passenger activates the ticket machine by <u>touching</u> the screen.
2 You answer the phone by _____ _____ the handset and _____ the green button.
3 The user starts the outboard motor by _____ the handle of the cord.
4 The rider starts the engine by _____ _____ the battery and _____ the lever downwards.
5 The burglar activated the alarm by _____ the laser beam.

SPEAKING »

3 Make questions and answers.

A: How does the passenger activate the ticket machine?
B: He activates it / He does it by touching the screen.

LANGUAGE »

Action	Method	
You start the outboard motor	by pulling	the cord.
The burglar activated the alarm	by breaking	the laser beam.

4 Work in pairs. Match the devices with the methods.

Device
1 accelerator on motorbike
2 voice-operated computer
3 solar battery
4 emergency stop in train
5 shop door alarm
6 car engine

How to start/activate it
a) put it under an electric lamp
b) step on a sensor in the door mat
c) rotate the handle
d) press and hold the remote start button
e) pull the lever
f) speak to it

SPEAKING »

5 Make questions and answers.

A: How do you activate the accelerator on a motorbike?
B: By rotating the handle. (or You activate it by rotating the handle.)

1 Action

WRITING »

6 Write sentences explaining how to activate or start the devices in 4.

> you   the user   the customer   the driver   the passenger

1 You activate / The user activates the accelerator on a motorbike by rotating the handle.

READING »

7 Look at this robot. What do you think it can do? How do you think it works? Discuss with your partner.

8 Read this article about another robot. Make notes. List all the actions it can do.

Examples: *climb stairs, walk sideways, avoid obstacles*

SPOT is the name of a four-legged, dog-like robot created by Boston Dynamics. Spot can climb stairs, walk on rough ground, inside or outside, and crawl into narrow spaces. It can walk forwards, backwards and sideways and it can turn round. It 'sees' and avoids holes and obstacles. (It 'thinks' anything over 30 cm high is an obstacle.) If it falls down, it can roll over and get up again. You can tell Spot where to go, but Spot will 'decide' how to get there.

How does it work? Each shoulder has three powerful motors which control the movements of the four legs in all directions. It can 'see' its environment by means of stereo cameras located at the front, rear and sides of its body. It can 'feel' the ground by pressure sensors in its legs. An operator can steer the robot by using a controller anywhere in the world, but powerful SLAM* software and processors *inside* the robot enable it to navigate to the location *autonomously*, that is, without input from the operator. A powerful battery located in Spot's lower body gives it a runtime of over 90 minutes.

*SLAM: simultaneous localisation and mapping

---

9 Read the article again. Complete the chart.

Spot can …	by means of …	located …
1 move its legs in all directions	12 motors	in its shoulders
2 operate for over 90 minutes	battery	
3 'see' things around it		around its body
4 'feel' the ground below it		
5 navigate to a location autonomously		inside the robot

10 Work in small groups. Discuss these questions.

1 In the reading text, the words *see, feel, decide* and *think* are in quotation marks (eg *Spot will 'decide' …*). Why?

2 With your group, make a list of possible uses for Spot. Then put them in order from most useful to least useful. Explain why. Are there any jobs that Spot should NOT be used for? Why?

11 Work in pairs. Prepare a list of questions to ask about Spot. Begin your questions with *What? How?* and *Where?*

12 Take turns to ask and answer the questions.

2 Work

1 Routines

An offshore oil drilling platform/rig

START HERE »

1 Would you like to work on an offshore oil platform? Why/Why not? Discuss with a partner.

LISTENING »

2 🔊 2.1 Tore and Ken work on different oil platforms. Listen to their phone call and complete the information on the left.

TORE	
ON DUTY: ___ weeks	
ON LEAVE: ___ weeks	
KEN	
ON DUTY: ___ weeks	
ON LEAVE: ___ weeks	

3 Listen to Tore (T) and Ken (K) again and complete the conversation.

T: Hi, Ken. How are things on your rig?
K: Hi, Tore. Well, we (1) _____ very hard at the moment. But I (2) _____ on leave tomorrow.
T: That's great. Where (3) _____? Back home?
K: I usually (4) _____ home to Nigeria. But this time I (5) _____ to France for a holiday.
T: Ah, fantastic. (6) _____ two weeks on, two weeks off?
K: No, I (7) _____ three on and three off. How about you?
T: I (8) _____ two two.
K: When's your next leave?
T: I'm on the helicopter right now! I (9) _____ to Norway!

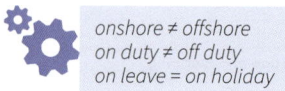

onshore ≠ offshore
on duty ≠ off duty
on leave = on holiday

LANGUAGE »

The present simple is used to talk about (1) regular or routine events; (2) job descriptions; (3) processes.

The present continuous is used to talk about (1) things happening now; (2) things happening temporarily around now; (3) plans or intentions for the near future.

SPEAKING »

4 Work in pairs. Ask each other about the changes in the work routine.

A: What does Tore usually do from six to seven forty-five?
B: He usually supervises the deck crew. But not today.
A: What's he doing today?
B: He's operating the main crane.

Changes to Monday morning duty roster for today only (because of staff illness)			
	06.00–07.45	08.00–09.45	10.00–10.45
BILLIE	~~inspect underwater pipes~~ check diving equipment	~~supervise divers~~ inspect blowout preventer	~~conduct safety drill~~ attend safety meeting
TORE	~~supervise deck crew~~ operate main crane	~~operate main crane~~ train new deck crew	~~work in control room~~ work on deck
ADELLE	~~check generators~~ repair power line	~~do maintenance work~~ supervise electricians	~~test electrical switches~~ write safety report

10 2 Work

5 🔊 2.2 Listen to these oil rig workers talking about their jobs on an offshore platform. Tick their jobs on the organisation charts.

6 Complete the job descriptions. Use the correct form of these verbs.

| maintain   operate   repair   report   supervise |

1 The Assistant Sub-Sea Engineer **repairs** and _____ the platform and the pipes under the sea. She _____ to the Sub-Sea Engineer.

2 The Assistant Crane Operator _____ and _____ the cranes on the main deck. He _____ to the Crane Operator.

3 The Assistant Driller _____ the drilling equipment. He _____ the Derrickhand and the Pumphand. He _____ to the Driller.

4 The Chief Electrician _____ and _____ all the electrical equipment on the rig. She _____ three electricians. She _____ to the Maintenance Supervisor.

SPEAKING »

7 Work in pairs. Act the parts of two of the oil rig workers. Ask each other about your jobs.

What's your job? What do you do?
I'm an Assistant Driller. I operate the drilling equipment.

Do you supervise anyone? Who do you supervise? Who reports to you?

Who do you report to? Who supervises you?

8 Write down your job title and a short job description. If you do not have a job, think of a job you want when you finish all your training.

9 Work in pairs. Ask each other about your jobs.

2 Plans

START HERE »

1. What jobs does a safety officer on an offshore oil platform have to do? Discuss with your partner.

LISTENING »

2. 🔊 2.3 Ben is a safety officer on an oil rig. Listen to his phone call. What is the purpose of the call?

   a) to discuss safety rules
   b) to talk about the strong wind
   c) to arrange a meeting

3. Listen to the phone call again and complete these notes.

   Day:
   Time:
   Participants:

   Agenda:

4. Listen to Tore (T) and Ben (B) again and fill in the gaps.

   T: Hello, Deck Crew. Tore speaking.
   B: Oh, hi Tore. This is Ben. How's it going?
   T: Not bad. But this strong wind is a problem for the cranes. Anyway, what can I do for you?
   B: I (1) _____ hold a meeting for the deck crew sometime soon.
   T: OK. What's the meeting (2) _____ be about?
   B: I (3) _____ tell them about the new safety rules for crane operators.
   T: OK, that's fine. When (4) _____ the meeting?
   B: How about three o'clock next Thursday?
   T: Yeah, that's great. Three o'clock next Thursday. See you then. Bye.
   B: Cheers. Bye.

LANGUAGE »

The present continuous, or *going to* + verb, is used to talk about plans or intentions.
I'm holding / I'm going to hold a meeting next Thursday.

to is used after verbs such as *plan, want, intend, hope*. *I want / intend / hope to finish this report next week.*

SPEAKING »

5. You are Ben and this is your diary for this week. Explain your plans.

Monday	Tuesday	Wednesday	Thursday	Friday
(1) 09.30 meet safety manager – discuss safety report	(3) 12.00 write new safety rules for cranes	(4) 08.00 inspect fire exits	(7) – day off!	(8) 09.30 write report about visit to Nord Platform
(2) 14.00 take helicopter to HQ – meet company manager		(5) 10.00 run fire drill		(9) 14.00 inspect sub-sea safety equipment
		(6) 14.00 visit Nord Platform – discuss new safety rules with manager		

Example: *On Monday at 9.30, I'm meeting the safety manager. We're going to discuss the safety report.*

6. Ask Ben questions about his diary.

   Example: *When are you meeting the safety manager? What are you going to discuss?*

TASK » **7** What things do you have to do today (or at the weekend)? Make a list and then work out a timetable for doing them. Present your plan to the class.

WRITING » **8** Rewrite this email replacing the phrases in italics.

To: Crane officer
From: Safety officer
Subject: Change to safety meeting
Cc: Safety manager

Thank you for your email this morning.

As you know, I have arranged a safety meeting for tomorrow.

I am sorry to inform you that I cannot attend the meeting. However, *I can confirm that* Bob will run the meeting.

I would be grateful if you could tell Tore about this change.

Please let me know if you need any further information.

I attach a copy of the agenda FYI.

Regards

Thanking	Thanks for; Many thanks for
Referring	With reference to; With regard to; Concerning
Reminding	As you are aware; As you may know; As you may be aware
Confirming	This is to confirm that; I'd like to confirm that; I confirm that
Bad news	I am sorry to tell you that; Unfortunately,
Good news	I am pleased to inform you that; Fortunately,
Informing	I would like to inform you that; This is to let you know that
Requesting	Please; Could you please; I would appreciate it if you could
Showing you are available	Please do not hesitate to contact me if; Do let me know if
Closing	Kind regards; Regards; Best wishes

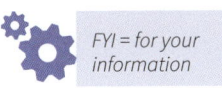

FYI = for your information

9 You are Pete. You work in customer services at Safety World. Reply to this email from Ben Brenner, safety officer at Nord Oil.

> Re: my online order no. 80832 for 3 × 30-metre ropes dated yesterday 14 Sept.
>
> Can you confirm that all your ropes are heat-resistant? How long is the guarantee?

- **thank:** Ben for his email today
- **remind him:** Safety World specialises in safety for oil platforms
- **confirm:** all the ropes you sell are heat-resistant and have five-year guarantees
- **request action:** decide about the order
- **show you are available:** to answer any further questions
- **attach:** a PDF giving information about the product

10 Exchange your emails with a partner. Take the part of Ben and reply to your partner's email.

- **thank:** Pete for his email yesterday
- **confirm:** you are happy with the guarantee and want to go ahead with the order
- **request action:** deliver as soon as possible
- **attach:** details of changed delivery address

3 New job

START HERE »   **1** Have you ever written a CV? What information goes into it?

READING »   **2** Read this printout of part of an online CV and answer the questions below.

PERSONAL INFORMATION	**Anna Petersons**	
	📞 +371 6678 9012	1
	📱 +371 2349 6587	2
	✉ anna.petersons29@dff.lv	3
JOB APPLIED FOR	**Senior audio maintenance technician**	4
WORK EXPERIENCE	**Audio maintenance technician**	5
from 2020 to present	Omega Studios, Riga, Latvia	6
from 2017 to 2019	I maintain digital audio equipment, make recordings, do troubleshooting and repairs and buy new equipment	7
	Sector: Electronics, entertainment, media	8
	Technician	9
	Comet Electronics, Riga, Latvia	10
	I repaired TV and video equipment	11
	Sector: Electronics	12
EDUCATION AND TRAINING	**Diploma in Audio Technology**	13
	Thames Valley University, London, UK	14
from 2019 to 2020	My subjects were: audio electronics, studio equipment, digital audio technology, editing, acoustics	15

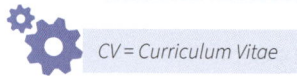
CV = Curriculum Vitae

1 What is Anna's surname?
2 What job does Anna want to have?
3 Where does Anna work now?
4 What is Anna's job description?
5 Where did Anna work in 2018?
6 What were Anna's responsibilities then?
7 What qualification does Anna have?
8 Where did Anna study?

SCANNING »   **3** Practise your speed reading. Look for the information you need on the SPEED SEARCH pages (118–119). Try to be the first to complete the task.

Task: Find an advert for a job relevant to Anna's career plans, qualifications and work experience.

LISTENING »   **4** Anna is talking about her CV. Fill in the gaps.

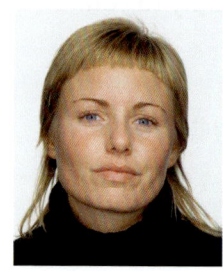

From 2017 until 2019, I (1) _____ at Comet Electronics as a technician. I (2) _____ Comet in 2019 and (3) _____ a full-time student at Thames Valley University in September 2019. From 2019 to 2020, I (4) _____ audio electronics at Thames Valley. In 2020, I (5) _____ my Diploma in Audio Technology. Then, in September 2020, I (6) _____ work as an audio maintenance technician at Omega Studios.

5 🔊 2.4 Listen to Anna and check your answers.

VOCABULARY »   **6**   Put these headings in the coloured boxes.

adjective   college subject   equipment   person   scientific concept

		noun			
1	en gin <u>eer</u>	<u>en</u> gine	en gin <u>eer</u> ing		
2	el ec tri cian			el ec tri ci ty	el ec tric al
3			el ec tron ics	el ec tron	el ec tron ic
4	mech an ic	mech an is m	mech an ics		mech an ic al
5	tech ni cian				tech ni cal
6	tech no lo gist		tech no lo gy		

7   Underline the stressed syllables in the words in the white boxes.

8   🔊 2.5   Listen and check your answers to 7.

9   Fill in the gaps.
1. The _____ is responsible for every _____ in the factory. (engineering/engineer/engine)
2. I'm a _____, but I want to become a _____ engineer. (mechanical/mechanic/mechanics)
3. The lab _____ maintains all the _____ equipment. (technician/technical/technology)
4. The _____ repairs all the _____ equipment on the rig. (electrical/electrician/electricity)

READING »   **10**   Write the numbers from the CV next to the questions to Anna.
a) What type of business do you work in? _____
b) Where are you working at the moment? _____
c) What's your job title? _____
d) When did you join Omega Studios? _____
e) What qualifications do you have in audio technology? _____
f) Where did you study for your diploma? _____
g) Where did you work before Omega Studios? _____

SPEAKING »   **11**   Work in pairs, A and B. Take turns to interview each other.
Student A: You are Anna. Answer questions about your CV.
Student B: You are the interviewer. Ask Anna questions about her CV.

TASK »   **12**   Write a short version of your CV.

13   Prepare for a job interview. Write notes in answer to these questions about a job you would like to apply for.
- Why do you want this job?
- What skills will you bring to this job?
- Why do you want to leave your present job?
- What questions would you like to ask the interviewers?

14   Work in small groups. Pass your CV around your group. Roleplay a job interview. Take turns to be interviewed by the rest of the group.

Review Unit A

1 Match the pictures with the instructions in the box.

> Pull it out.   Push them down.   Push it forward.   Put it in.   Pull it back.
> Pour it in.   Take it off.   Pick them up.   Switch it on.   Take them out.
> Take it away.   Put it on.   Pour it out.   Switch it off.   Put them down.   Push it in.

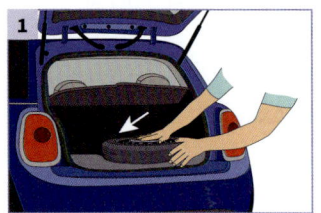 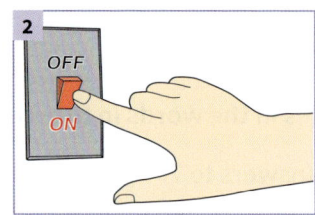  
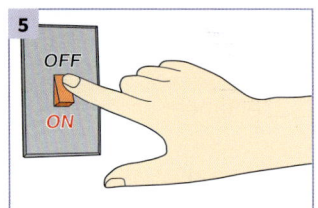 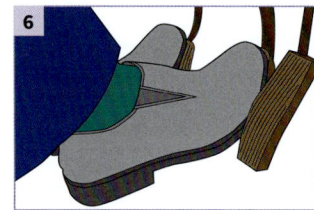 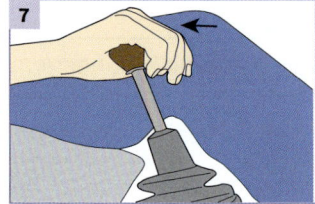 
  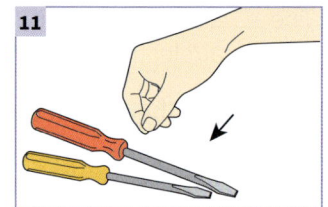 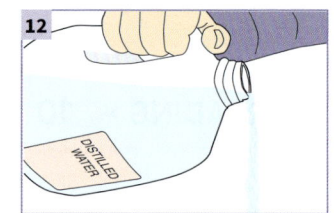
 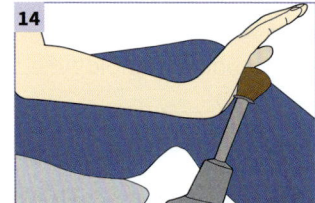  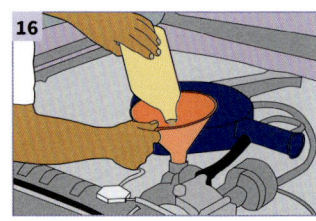

2 Complete these dialogues.

1 **A:** *Have you* <u>switched off</u> *the engine yet?* (switch off)
  B: *No, not yet. I'm* <u>switching it off</u> *now.*
2 **A:** *Has she _____ the jack yet?* (bring out)
  B: *No, she hasn't. Look, she's _____ now.*
3 **A:** *Has he _____ the wheel nuts yet?* (take off)
  B: *No, not yet. I think he's _____ at the moment.*
4 **A:** *Have you _____ the new wheels yet?* (put on)
  B: *Hold on. I'm _____ right now.*
5 **A:** *Have the mechanics _____ the jacks yet?* (take away)
  B: *Not yet, but I think they're _____ now.*
6 **A:** *Has Bill _____ the spark plugs yet?* (put back)
  B: *I don't think so. I think he's _____ now.*

3   **Complete this progress report by the car mechanic (M) to her supervisor (S).**

S: *Have you checked the tyres yet?*
M: Yes, we (1) <u>checked</u> (check) all the tyres first thing this morning and we (2) _____ (find) that the rear OS tyre was worn. So we (3) _____ (replace) it.
S: *What about the tyre pressures? Have you adjusted them yet?*
M: Yes, we (4) _____ (adjust) them when we (5) _____ (put) the tyres on. Then, at about ten this morning, we (6) _____ (examine) the fuel system. We (7) _____ (take) it apart and (8) _____ (unblock) the fuel pipe.
S: *Good. Have you repaired the damaged paintwork on the door?*
M: Yes, we (9) _____ (strip) off the damaged paint just before lunch and then straight after lunch, we (10) _____ (clean) the door, (11) _____ (repair) it and (12) _____ (repaint) it.
S: *Good. Now what about the air conditioner? Have you checked it?*
M: Yes, we checked it at about three this afternoon. Then we (13) _____ (pump) some new fluid into the air conditioning system.
S: *What about the oil leak under the car? Have you had time to look at that yet?*
M: Yes, we (14) _____ (do) that about an hour ago.

4   **Complete these statements with the correct forms of words in the box.**

| loosen operate hold keep look stop switch |
| protect put raise shield wear |

1 The driver <u>shields</u> his eyes from dust by <u>looking</u> through the visor on his helmet.
2 The wheel gun mechanics _____ the wheel nuts by _____ their wheel guns.
3 The wheel jack guys _____ the whole car by _____ jacks under the front and rear.
4 Mechanics _____ the car steady by _____ it with their hands.
5 The mechanics _____ themselves from fire by _____ fire suits.
6 A safety mechanic can _____ the car by _____ the light to red.

5   **The chart shows part of the organisation of an oil rig. Make sentences about it, using the words in the box.**

| manage report to supervise work for |

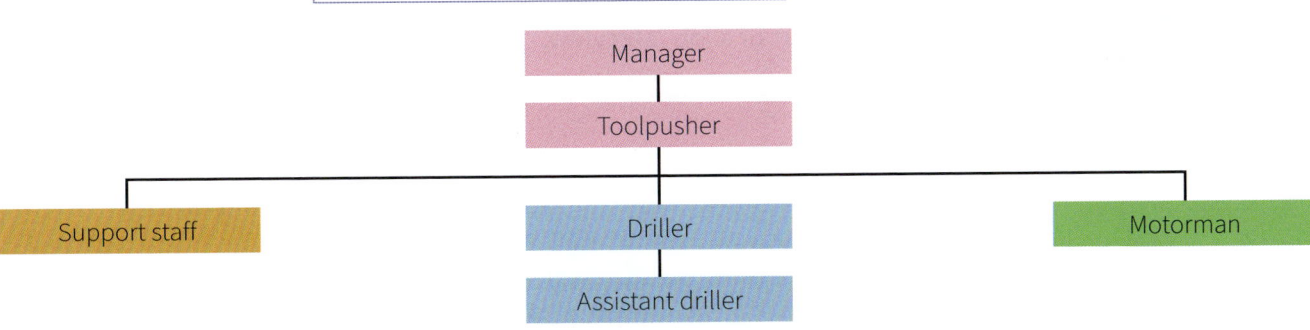

6 Complete this job description with the correct form of the words in the box.

check have inspect make maintain order repair report supervise work

CHIEF MECHANIC ON THE NORD OIL PLATFORM
JOB DESCRIPTION

The Chief Mechanic is part of the support staff on the Nord Oil Platform and is responsible for maintaining all the mechanical equipment on the rig. He/She (1) <u>maintains</u> the diesel generators and (2) _____ every machine on the platform. He/She (3) _____ all the equipment daily, and (4) _____ sure that all machines are in good working order. He/She (5) _____ broken equipment and (6) _____ replacement parts and new tools. Most of the time he/she (7) _____ outside or on deck. The Chief Mechanic (8) _____ to the rig Toolpusher and (9) _____ a small crew of two assistant mechanics and two motormen. He/She normally (10) _____ a two weeks on/two weeks off schedule.

7 Work in pairs, A and B. Have a phone conversation to arrange a meeting with each other.

Use different structures and verbs: *I'm attending …/I'm going to …/I'm planning to …*

A's plans for next week

| MON pm – arrange visit of customers to site |
| TUE am – go to computer training course |
| WED pm – show customers around site |
| THU am – meet new staff |

B's plans for next week

| MON am – attend project meeting |
| TUE pm – run training course for staff |
| WED am – inspect damaged warehouse |
| THU am – visit trade fair |

A: *Are you free on Monday morning?*
B: *No, I'm sorry I'm not. I'm attending a project meeting. How about Monday afternoon?*

8 Practise your speed reading. Look for the information you need on the SPEED SEARCH pages (118–119). Try to be the first to complete the task.

Task: Find this advice about job interviews:
- one thing you should do *before* your interview
- one thing you should do *at* your interview
- one thing you should *not* do at your interview

9 Complete this part of a job interview.
- *Where* (1) _____? (you/work)
- I work at Central Telecoms. I'm a technician there.
- *How long* (2) _____ there? (you/be)
- (3) _____ there for two years. (I/be)
- *And where* (4) _____ before that? (you/work)
- Before that (5) _____ a junior technician at MobileForce. (I/be)
- *Why* (6) _____ MobileForce? (you/leave)
- Because (7) _____ to work in a bigger company. (I/want)
- (8) _____ your part-time diploma? (you/finish)
- Yes, I have.
- *When* (9) _____ it? (you/complete)
- Last July.

10 **Identify the devices from their descriptions.**

1 This device sells rail or bus tickets to travellers. The traveller activates it by touching the screen.
2 This device sounds an alarm when an intruder enters a building. The burglar activates it by interrupting a laser beam.
3 This machine is located on the rear of a motorboat. The sailor starts it by pulling a handle. The handle is attached to a cord (or cable).
4 This device makes a motorbike go faster. You activate it by twisting the handle on the handlebars.

11 **Correct the mistakes in these sentences.**

1 My brother is a mechanism. He studied mechanical at technique college.
2 We need to find a good electricity to repair the electrician wires in the house.
3 I'm a computer technical. How can I help you?
4 I'm studying for a diploma in electronic. I want to be an electron engineer.

12 **Rewrite this email. Replace words/phrases in italics with ones from this list. Make any necessary changes to punctuation.**

best wishes; this is to let you know; I'd be grateful if you would; with reference to

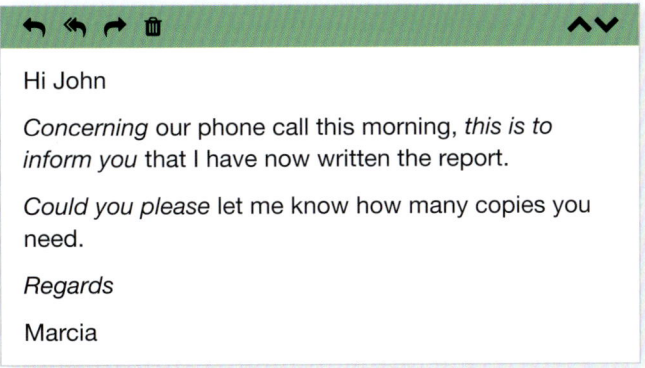

Hi John

Concerning our phone call this morning, *this is to inform you* that I have now written the report.

Could you please let me know how many copies you need.

Regards

Marcia

PROJECT » **13** **Start work on a full version of your own CV.**

- Refer to the Europass template on the internet. (Key *Europass CV* into a search engine.)
- Write a first draft. Remember to update it when your information changes.

Note: if you have not yet worked in a full-time job, write about part-time or holiday jobs in the Work Experience section of the CV.

14 **Research a job you are interested in.**

- Collect interesting job adverts. Make a list of the skills you will need.
- Find out more about the job.
- Find out about some companies that you are interested in.
- Write a description of the job you want.
- Put all the information you have collected into a special folder.

3 Comparison

1 Limits

START HERE » 1 What do these road signs tell you?

LISTENING » 2 🔊 3.1 A customer wants to drive their car onto a car ferry. Listen to their phone conversation with the sales staff of the ferry company. Complete the approximate specifications of the customer's vehicle on the left.

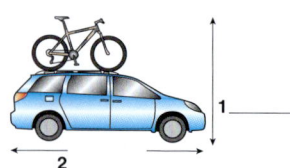

Roof rack

3 Listen again and complete the conversation between the salesperson (S) and the customer (C).

S: How (1) _____ ?
C: It's just under (2) _____ metres wide.
S: OK, that's fine. The vehicle must not be (3) _____ 2 metres.
C: Great.
S: (4) _____ ?
C: It's exactly (5) _____ metres long.
S: Please measure it again carefully. It must not be (6) _____ 7 metres.
C: OK, I'll do that and get back to you.
S: (7) _____ ?
C: It's just over (8) _____ metres high, including the bicycles.
S: Mm, that's too high. The vehicle must not be (9) _____ 2.9 metres.
C: OK, I'll take the bikes off.

READING » 4 Read the SeaFerry web page. Which vehicles on the left can board the ferry? What are the vehicle types (*large car, standard car,* etc.)?

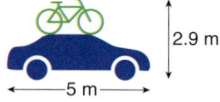

SeaFerry is a cars-only service: we do not take coaches or lorries.

WEIGHT AND DIMENSION LIMITS FOR ALL VEHICLES
Vehicles must not be heavier than 3.5 tonnes. They must not be wider than 2.0 m, longer than 7.0 m or higher than 2.9 m.
STANDARD CAR: A 'standard car' must not be longer than 5.0 m, wider than 2.0 m or higher than 1.85 m. It must carry a maximum of five passengers. If it carries more than five persons, it becomes a 'large car'.
LARGE CAR: A 'large car' must not be longer than 7.0 m, wider than 2.0 m or higher than 2.9 m. It must carry no more than nine passengers.
HIGH CAR: A 'high car' must not be higher than 2.9 m, longer than 5.0 m or wider than 2.0 m. It must carry a maximum of five passengers. This vehicle type allows passengers to put extra luggage on the roof of their cars, within the limits.
CAR AND TRAILER: A car and trailer must not be longer than 7.0 m, higher than 2.9 m or wider than 2.0 m. It must carry no more than nine passengers over the age of three.

LANGUAGE »

The comparative form of single-syllable adjectives ends in *-er*, e.g. *longer, wider*. Two-syllable adjectives ending in *-y* also end in *-er*, e.g. *noisy → noisier*.

Notice the spelling changes: *big → bigger*; *wide → wider*; *easy → easier*.
than is used after the comparative adjective, e.g. *The van is higher than the car*.
Irregular comparatives: *better, worse, farther/further, more* and *less*.
more + adjective is used with adjectives of more than one syllable, e.g. *more expensive*. *less* is used with all types of adjective, e.g. *less cheap, less expensive*.
If something is the wrong dimension for something, or above a limit, you can say:
The lorry is too wide for the bridge. The bridge is not wide enough for the lorry.

5 Explain the problem.

The bridge is 2.7 metres high, but the lorry is 2.9 metres high. The lorry is too high for the bridge.

1. height of bridge: 2.7 m; height of lorry: 2.9 m
2. width of ship: 12.2 m; width of canal: 11.5 m
3. length of plane: 19.3 m; length of hangar: 18.8 m
4. diameter of disc brake: 172 mm; width of box: 160 mm
5. thickness of coin: 3 mm; width of slot: 2.88 mm
6. length of screw: 5.5 cm; length of hole: 4.35 cm

TASK »

6 Work in pairs. Read the text, then discuss the invention. Do you think people will buy it? Give your reasons. Make notes of your discussion.

- Compare it with (a) a normal car and (b) a small aircraft.
- List (a) its strengths and (b) its weaknesses.

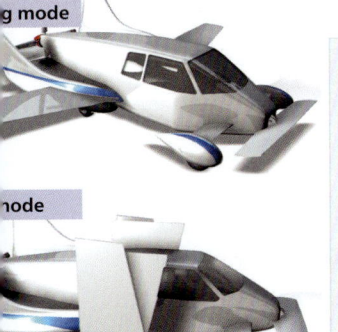

The road-ready plane

You can park it in your garage, drive it to your nearest airfield, fly it to your destination, land it, then drive off the runway, along a road to your workplace. In the air, it has a wingspan of 8.4 m, a length of 5.7 m and a height of 2 m. It can fly at a speed of 185 km/h for 740 km on a single tank of fuel. The tank holds 76 litres of super-unleaded petrol. In car mode, it can go 17 km per litre of fuel and can travel faster than normal car cruising speeds, but it has only two seats and no space for luggage. The cost of the road-ready plane is approximately £300,000.

WRITING »

7 Work individually. Reply to this email from your company director. Use the notes from your discussion.

Hi Bob

What do you think about the road-ready plane? Could you put a few ideas in an email to me? Perhaps you can use these headings:

1 What it can do; 2 What it can't do; 3 Comparison with a small plane; 4 Comparison with a car; 5 Main strengths; 6 Main weaknesses; 7 Recommendation (that is, should we buy one for our company executives?).

Thanks
Rita

2 Products

START HERE »

1 **Which features are most important to you in a mobile phone? List them in order of importance. Compare your list with your partner's.**

Here are some examples: *size of phone, screen size, camera quality, recharging speed, storage capacity, weight, water resistance, number of speakers.* Think of other features.

LISTENING »

2 🔊 3.2 **Listen and complete the details in the customer call record.**

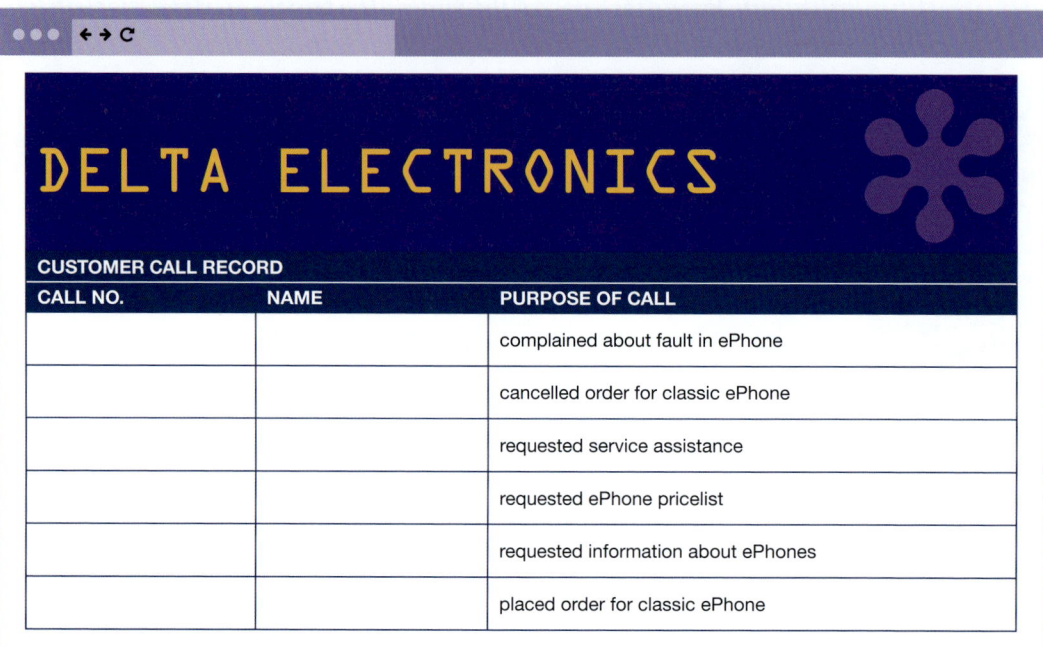

DELTA ELECTRONICS

CUSTOMER CALL RECORD

CALL NO.	NAME	PURPOSE OF CALL
		complained about fault in ePhone
		cancelled order for classic ePhone
		requested service assistance
		requested ePhone pricelist
		requested information about ePhones
		placed order for classic ePhone

3 **Listen again and complete the sentences.**

1 Sorry, _____ you repeat that, please? (Phone call 1)
2 _____ I have your name, please? (Phone call 2)
3 I _____ like to cancel an order, please. (Phone call 3)
4 _____ you think you _____ tell me the model number, please? (Phone call 3)
5 I _____ like some information about the ePhone, please. (Phone call 4)
6 _____ you like me _____ email you the specifications? (Phone call 4)
7 _____ I put you through to the service department? (Phone call 5)
8 _____ you mind _____ me what the problem is? (Phone call 6)

4 **Match the sentences from 3 with these language functions.**

a) saying what you want _____
b) offering to do something _____
c) asking someone to do something _____
d) checking information _____

SPEAKING »

5 **Work in pairs. Roleplay phone conversations between customer and service staff. Practise the six dialogues. Use the customer call record in 2.**

Study the Audio script on pages 121–122 before you begin.

6 Look at the chart and complete this phone conversation.

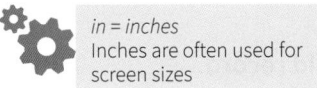
in = inches
Inches are often used for screen sizes

Comparison between two smartphones: the Fonarama 11 and the Classic 5.1		
	Fonarama 11	Classic 5.1
Dimensions	150.9 × 75.7 × 8.3 mm	151.7 × 69.1 × 7.9 mm
Weight	194 g	163 g
Screen size	6.1 in	6.2 in
Battery life	'all day'	'all day'
Charging speed	7.5W wireless	15W wireless
Price	£785	£805

A: What's the difference between the Fonarama 11 and the Classic 5.1?
B: Well, the Classic is much (1) _____ and (2) _____ than the Fonarama. It's only 7.9 mm thick and 69.1 mm wide.
A: I see. And what about the weight?
B: Well, again, the Classic is much (3) _____ than the Fonarama. It weighs only 163 g.
A: OK, and what about the screen size?
B: The screen of the Classic is slightly (4) _____. It's 6.2 inches diagonally.
A: That's good. What about battery life and charging speed?
B: Well, their battery life is the same, but the Classic has a (5) _____ charging speed at 15W wireless.
A: OK, I've decided I'll order the grey Classic one.

7 Practise the conversation.

8 Which word does *one* refer to in this dialogue?

A: I'd like to buy a plastic case for my smartphone, please.
B: Which one would you like? Do you want the white one or the black one?
A: The black one, please.

LANGUAGE »

one is used when someone has already mentioned a thing, there is a choice between two or more types of the thing and you don't want to repeat the name of the thing.

A: Please pass me a spanner.
B: Which one do you want? The long one or the short one?

Speaker B wants to mention two types of spanner, but does not want to repeat the word *spanner*.

SPEAKING »

9 The word *one* is missing from four places in this dialogue. Mark the places.

A: Hello, I'd like to buy a DAB radio, please.
B: Certainly. We have two colours, red or black and there are two models. There's with Bluetooth streaming and there's without Bluetooth. Which would you like?
A: I'd like the red with Bluetooth, please.

10 🔊 3.3 Listen and check your answers.

11 Practise the corrected dialogue with your partner. Use these notes.

DAB radio

model: with or without Bluetooth streaming / **colour:** red or black

3 Equipment

START HERE »

1 Work in small groups. Discuss these questions about each world record.

- Is it still a world record? If not, what is the new record?
- If it is still a record, how long will it last? Why?

1 The fastest woman in the world is Florence Griffith Joyner. She ran 100 m in 10.49 seconds.
2 The world's tallest building is the Burj Khalifa in Dubai, at 828 m.
3 The world's smallest transistor is only the size of a single atom of metal.
4 The longest stay in space was 437 days by Valeri Polyakov.

READING »

2 Jeff and Zara work in a company that provides motorboats for hire to tourists. Read their email correspondence and answer the questions.

To: Chief engineer
From: Manager, Motorboat Fleet
Subject: Tender for purchase of new outboard engines

Jeff

As you know, we're going to replace all our outboard engines. Could you please test five engines from different suppliers? Let me know the cheapest and the best performance.

Thanks. Zara.

To: Manager, Motorboat Fleet
From: Chief engineer
Subject: Re: Tender for purchase of new outboard engines

Hi Zara

Thanks for your email. I can confirm that we've finished the tests on the five engines. I'm attaching specs and test results. I'll send you a full report in a couple of days.

Cheers. Jeff.

1 What is the purpose of (a) the first email (b) the second email?
2 In the first email, what does Zara (a) remind Jeff about (b) want Jeff to do?
3 In the second email, (a) what new information does Jeff tell Zara (b) what does Jeff promise to do?

SCANNING »

3 Practise your speed reading. Look for the information you need on the SPEED SEARCH pages (118–119). Try to be the first to complete the task.

Task: Underline the correct answers below.

Specifications
1 Engine A has a (*shorter/longer*) shaft than Engine B.
2 The heaviest engine is Engine (*A/B/C/D/E*).
3 Engine D is the (*cheapest/most expensive*) engine.
4 Engine C is (*as powerful as/more powerful than/less powerful than*) Engine E.

Test results

1 The (*fastest/slowest*) engine was Engine C.
2 The (*most rapid/least rapid*) acceleration from 0–40 km/h was Engine C.
3 The (*quietest/noisiest*) engine was Engine B.
4 The engine with the lowest fuel consumption was Engine (*A/B/C/D/E*).

LANGUAGE » To change the comparative into the superlative form, change *-er* to *-est*, *more* to *most* and *less* to *least*, e.g. *longest, widest, biggest, noisiest, most expensive, least noisy*.

the is used in front of the superlative, e.g. *the fastest car in the world*.

There are five irregular superlatives: *best, worst, farthest/furthest, most* and *least*.

SPEAKING » **4 Make comparisons. Think of as many differences as possible. Think of some more groups and make comparisons.**

1 tablet / laptop / smartphone
2 concrete / steel / glass
3 coal-fired power / nuclear power / wind power
4 phone calls / video conferencing / in-person meetings

5 Work in pairs. Write down three items or products you know about. Compare them and make notes.

TASK » **6 Work in small groups. Have a meeting to discuss this problem and agree on the best solution.**

You and the other members of your group work on an oil rig in a desert. The rig is about 130 km from the nearest town. The town has a small airport. There is no road between the town and the rig and an aircraft cannot land at the rig. Between the town and the rig, the land is sandy and rocky, with some hills. Your team needs to transport small teams of three to six engineers and to tow a trailer with heavy drilling equipment between the airport and the rig. Your team wants to buy a 4 × 4 with the following features:

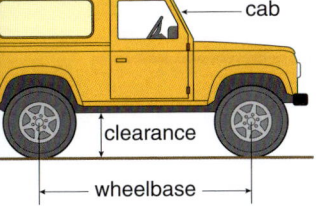

4 × 4 = four wheel drive
say: four by four

- long wheelbase
- high clearance
- powerful engine
- space for up to six passengers
- low fuel consumption
- large fuel tank
- towing power (able to pull other vehicles)
- high cab (to allow driver to see easily)
- low price

Student A: your information is on page 111. **Student C:** your information is on page 115.
Student B: your information is on page 113. **Student D:** your information is on page 117.

WRITING » **7 Work individually. Write a short report on your meeting. Give your group's decision and the reasons for the decision. Use these headings.**

1	Introduction
	Our team held a meeting yesterday to choose …
2	Comparison of four vehicles
	We compared the specifications of the four vehicles:
	1.1 The Jeep Grand Cherokee has the longest wheelbase. It is 2915 mm in length.
	1.2 …
3	Decision
	We decided to buy the _____ because …

3 Comparison 25

4 Processes

1 Infrastructure

START HERE » 1 What is this? What does it do? How does it work? Discuss with your partner.

LISTENING » 2 🔊 4.1 Listen and complete the chart.

Name of TBM:	
Length (m)	
Diameter at start (m)	
Diameter at finish (m)	
Tunneling speed (m/day)	

READING » 3 Read this article and match these headings to the correct paragraph.

Collecting   Moving
Cutting   Strengthening

Hard-rock tunnel boring machines

1 The large, circular cutter head contains rotating disc cutters, which act like sharp teeth. Some cutter heads can have 80 or more disc cutters. When the head rotates, the teeth cut large circles into the surface of the rock until the rock breaks.

2 Pieces of rock fall to the ground. They are collected by large buckets around the edge of the cutter head. When the cutter head rotates upwards, the rocks fall by gravity onto a conveyor belt. They are then carried to the rear of the machine.

3 First, the gripper shoes move outwards and grip the tunnel wall. Then, the propel cylinders push the whole machine forwards. Next, the legs push downwards against the tunnel floor to support the machine. Now, the shoes move back from the wall. Next, the shoes are pulled forwards by the propel cylinders. Finally, the shoes move outwards to grip the next section of wall and the legs are pulled back up from the tunnel floor.

4 There are two drills located behind the cutter head. When the machine moves forwards, holes are drilled into the roof of the tunnel. Then, the holes are filled with bolts and cement. This makes the roof stronger.

4 Read paragraph 3 again. Put the numbered actions (A–F) in the correct order. There are seven actions.

A shoes move out (x2)   C legs move down   E machine moves forward
B shoes move in   D legs move up   F shoes move forward

VOCABULARY » 5 Make a list of all the names of parts of the body and clothing in the text in 3.

6 List other technical contexts where the items in 5 are used.

Example: 'teeth' are also found on gears.

LANGUAGE » In an active sentence, the subject = the agent. The subject does the action.

Subject = agent	Active verb	Object
Propel cylinders	push	the machine.
Large buckets	collect	the rocks.

In a passive sentence, the subject is NOT the same as the agent. The subject does not do the action. The agent does the action to the subject.

Subject	Passive verb		Agent
	be	Past participle	
The machine	is	pushed	by propel cylinders.
The rocks	are	collected	by large buckets.

6 Change this set of instructions into a description of a process, using the passive and the words in the box.

finally   first   next   now   then

How to change the oil in a car

1 Run the engine for a few minutes.
2 Switch off the engine.
3 Take off the oil drain plug.
4 Empty the old oil into a container.
5 Put the oil drain plug on.
6 Take off the oil filler cap.
7 Pour in the new oil.
8 Put the oil filler cap back on.

Begin: First, the engine is run for a few minutes. Then, it is switched off. Now, the …

7 Make a set of instructions about a process you know about. Then rewrite it as a process description in the passive.

Examples of processes: food manufacture, steel making, canning, assembling computer components, mixing concrete, dairy processing.

8 Fill in the gaps, using the correct form of the verbs in brackets.

1 Large drills _____ (make) holes in the roof of the tunnel. Then, the holes _____ (fill) with bolts and cement.
2 A large propeller _____ (push) the hovercraft forwards. The propeller _____ (drive) by a powerful engine.
3 Hot water _____ (flow) from the engine into the radiator. Here it _____ (cool) by the fan.
4 The robot _____ (monitor) by a computer. This computer also _____ (control) all the other robots in the building.
5 First, the rusty machine parts _____ (bring) into the factory. Then, they _____ (clean). Then, the rust _____ (remove). Next, the parts _____ (paint). Finally, they _____ (take) out of the factory again.

9 Make a list of headings for the main stages of a process you know about. Make each heading begin with a verb ending in *-ing*, like the ones in 3.

Example: *Moulding and shaping steel – 1 Melting the steel; 2 Casting; 3 Cooling; 4 Rolling the steel; 5 Straightening; 6 Cutting.*

10 Give a short talk to the class explaining your process. Use your headings.

2 Manufacturing

START HERE »

1. What do you know about cars? Discuss with a partner the location and function of these parts: *body, chassis, drive shaft, axle, transmission*.

2. The pictures show the main stages in assembling a car, but they are in the wrong order. Write the figure numbers in the correct boxes in the flow chart.

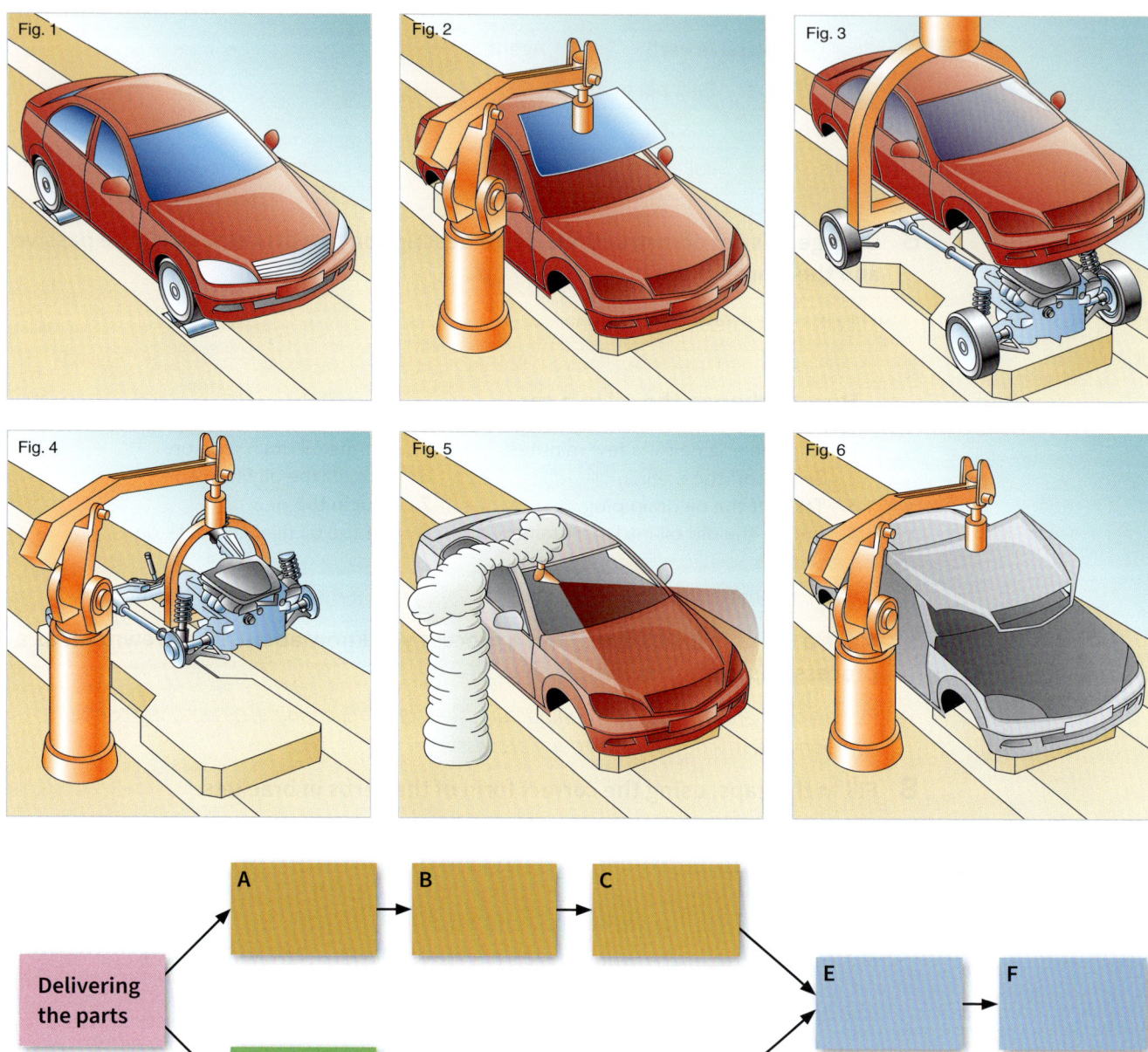

3. Make captions for the six pictures with the verbs and nouns in the box. Use verbs ending in *-ing*.

| add   attach   install   paint   test   weld   body   chassis   finished car   parts |

Example: *Fig 6. Welding the body panels to the body frame*

28 4 Processes

READING » **4** Read this website of a car company and check your answers to 2 and 3.

Assembling a car

First, the parts are delivered by truck or rail to the *delivery area* of the car assembly plant. From here, some parts are taken to the body shop and other parts are transported to the chassis line. The parts are carried around the plant by forklift trucks or conveyor belts.

In the *body shop*, the panels are welded to the frame to form the body of the car. This is done by more than 400 robots.

Then, the body is taken to the *paint shop*. Here it is cleaned and painted by robots. Special clothing is worn by the robots to protect the paint. After this, the body is checked by human workers to look for faults.

Next, the painted body moves along a conveyor belt to the *trim line* and many parts are added to it. For example, the instrument panel, the air conditioning system, the heating system and the electrical wiring are all installed here. The windscreen is inserted by robots using laser guides.

Meanwhile, in the *chassis line*, components are added to the chassis. First, the chassis is turned upside down, to make the work easier. Then, the fuel system, the transmission, the suspension, the exhaust system, the axles and the drive shaft are all installed. Next, the chassis is turned over (rightside up). The engine is lowered into the chassis and connected to it.

Now, the chassis and the body move simultaneously to the *final assembly line*. Here, the body is attached to the chassis and all the final parts are added. The tyres and the radiator are added here. The hoses are connected, and the radiator and air conditioner are filled with fluid. The car's central computer is also installed here.

Lastly, the finished car and all electrical systems are tested. The car is filled with fuel and the engine is started for the first time. The car is put on special rollers to test the engine and the wheels. If it passes the test, the car is finally driven out of the assembly plant.

LANGUAGE » **to + verb** is used to talk or write about the purpose of an action.

Why do you paint the car body? To protect it from rust.
The car body is painted to protect it from rust.

SPEAKING » **5** Match actions with their purposes. Refer to the text in 4.

action
1 workers weld thin metal sheets to a frame
2 they turn the chassis upside down
3 the robots wear special clothes
4 they turn the chassis rightside up
5 workers put the finished car on rollers
6 workers check the car body by hand

purpose of action
a) to check the movement of the wheels
b) to make the car body
c) to inspect it for faults in the paint
d) to protect the wet paint from dust
e) to install the fuel system more easily
f) to lower the engine into it

6 In pairs, ask and answer the questions in 5. Use the passive form in the question.

A: Why are thin metal sheets welded to a frame?
B: To make the car body.

7 Ask questions to get these answers. Refer to the text in 4.

1 They're delivered by truck or rail.
2 They're welded together in the body shop.
3 They're carried by forklift trucks or conveyor belts.
4 To look for faults in the paint.
5 It's done by human workers.
6 It's done using laser guides.

3 Communications

START HERE »

1 What do you know about communications satellites? Do this quiz with your partner. All the numbers are approximate. Choose the answer closest to the correct one.

   1 How high are communications satellites above the Earth?
      a) 15,000 km   b) 25,000 km   c) 35,000 km   d) 45,000 km
   2 How fast do these satellites travel around the Earth?
      a) 7000 km/h   b) 11,000 km/h   c) 15,000 km/h   d) 21,000 km/h
   3 What frequency are signals from a communications satellite to your satellite dish?
      a) 12 GHz   b) 1.2 GHz   c) 12 MHz   d) 1.2 MHz
   4 What frequency are the signals from your satellite dish to your TV?
      a) 150 MHz   b) 1500 MHz   c) 15 GHz   d) 150 GHz

SCANNING »

2 Practise your speed reading. Look for the information you need on the SPEED SEARCH pages (118–119). Try to be the first to complete this task.

   Task: Check your answers to the quiz in 1.

READING »

3 Read this instruction leaflet and match the words in the box with the numbers (1–7) in the diagram.

   | coaxial cable   satellite dish   satellite receiver   LNB   satellite   TV   transmitter dish |

How to set up your satellite TV

Equipment needed

You will need a TV and separate satellite receiver, or a TV with a built-in satellite receiver.
5 This is connected by a coaxial cable to a satellite dish on your house, which should be at least 60 cm in diameter, preferably larger for good reception. The dish must have a low noise block (LNB). This converts high-frequency
10 signals to low-frequency ones.

How it works

There is a communications satellite in orbit high above the Earth. TV programmes are transmitted as radio signals from a transmitter dish up to the satellite, which then sends the signals down to Earth. These signals have a high frequency of several GHz (see diagram).
15 Your dish receives the high-frequency signals and reflects them to the LNB, which then converts the signal into a lower frequency (see diagram).
The LNB is connected via the coaxial cable to the satellite receiver, which processes the signal. It extracts the video and audio and plays them as TV programmes via the TV set. If your TV has a built-in satellite receiver, the signal will go directly from the LNB to the TV set.

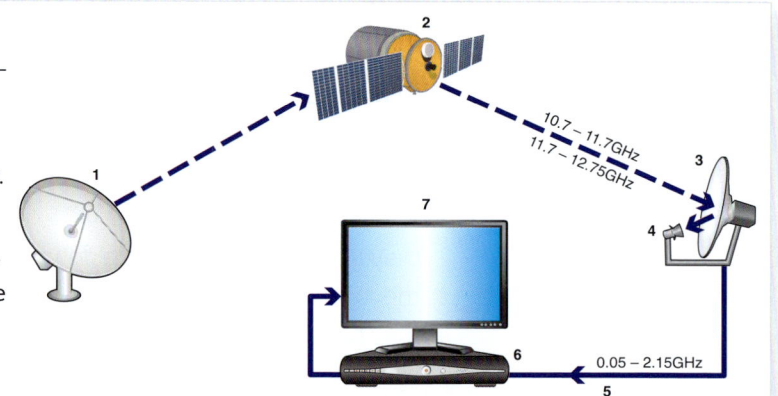

via = by means of

4 What does *which* refer to in the text?

   1 line 6   a) cable   b) satellite dish
   2 line 13   a) satellite   b) transmitter dish
   3 line 15   a) frequency   b) LNB
   4 line 17   a) satellite receiver b) cable

4 Processes

LANGUAGE »

| Signals are transmitted to | the satellite. The satellite / the satellite, which | then sends the signals to Earth. |

| John reports to | Adel. Adel / Adel, who | is the training manager. |

5 Join these pairs of sentences. Use *who* or *which*.

1 My smart TV has a built-in satellite receiver. This is connected by cable to my satellite dish.
2 If your receiver doesn't work, contact our technician. He will repair it.
3 The dish reflects the signal to the LNB. This converts the signal to a lower frequency.
4 Please send any complaints to our customer service manager. She will then contact you.
5 The radio station sends signals to the satellite. This then transmits the signals to my dish.
6 My satellite receiver extracts the audio and video. These are then displayed on my TV set.

Example: *1 My smart TV has a built-in satellite receiver, which is connected by cable to my satellite dish.*

VOCABULARY »

6 Match words with the same or similar meaning.

| transmit   receive   convert   extract   display   operate | get   send   take out   change   work   show |

7 Complete the sentences. Notice the hyphens (-).

1 The signal has a high frequency. It's a <u>high-frequency</u> signal.
2 This pump uses high pressure. It's a _____ pump.
3 The fuse breaks at 13 amps. It's a <u>13-amp</u> fuse. (Note: amps ➔ amp)
4 The cable carries 13,800 volts. It's a _____ cable.
5 My satellite dish is 1.8 metres wide. It's a _____ dish.

SPEAKING »

8 Draw a simple diagram and make notes about a setup you know. If you prefer, use this satellite dish setup and make notes about the diagram.

9 Describe the setup and explain to the class how it works.

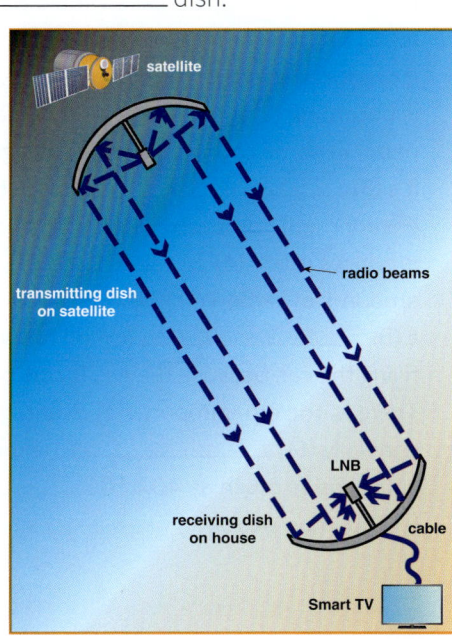

4 Processes 31

Review Unit B

1 Choose two of these cars and make comparisons between them.

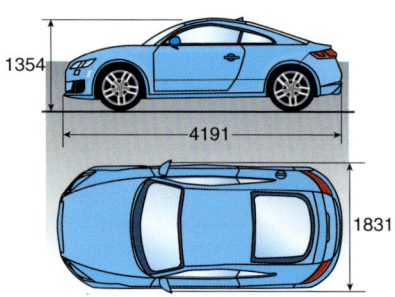
1354
4191
1831

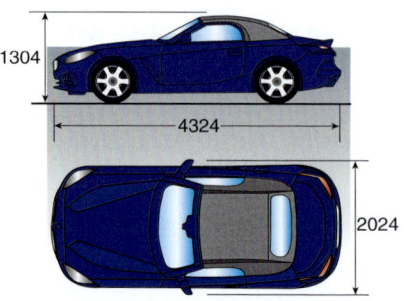
1304
4324
2024

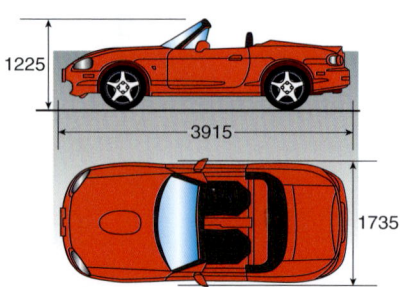
1225
3915
1735

Car 1: the Audi TT Coupe	
Fuel tank capacity	66 L
Engine size	2.0 L
Top speed	130 mph
Acceleration	0 to 60 mph: 5.3 sec.
Fuel consumption	31.0 mpg
CO^2 emission	167 g/km

Car 2: the BMW Z4 Roadster	
Fuel tank capacity	52 L
Engine size	2.0 L
Top speed	149 mph
Acceleration	0 to 62 mph: 6.6 sec.
Fuel consumption	39.2 mpg
CO^2 emission	163 g/km

Car 3: the Mazda MX-5 Convertible	
Fuel tank capacity	45 L
Engine size	1.5 L
Top speed	127 mph
Acceleration	0 to 60 mph: 8.3 sec.
Fuel consumption	44.8 mpg
CO^2 emission	171 g/km

2 Compare all three cars. Say which one you like best and why.

3 Complete the text.

Which is the better fuel for internal combustion engines? Is there a cleaner and (1) <u>greener</u> (green) fuel than petrol? A fuel called liquid petroleum gas (LPG) can make cars go as fast as petrol, although it produces less energy per litre. However, LPG is becoming (2) <u>more popular</u> (popular) than petrol in some countries because it's greener: it's (3) _____ (harmful) to the environment compared with petrol because LPG produces much (4) _____ (low) amounts of carbon dioxide than petrol. LPG is also a (5) _____ (clean) fuel when you're filling the car, because the gas is completely sealed. There is one other important advantage of LPG: it's generally (6) _____ (expensive), in some countries as much as 40% (7) _____ (cheap) than petrol.

But if you want to help the environment even more, the (8) <u>greenest</u> (green) type of fuel for a car is electricity. Compared with both petrol and LPG vehicles, the engine of an electric vehicle (EV) is the (9) <u>most efficient</u> (efficient) and the (10) _____ (easy) to maintain. One reason for this is that an EV engine has (11) _____ (few) moving parts compared with petrol or LPG-fuelled vehicles. EVs are also the (12) _____ (expensive) to operate: a petrol car, for example, may cost 2–3 times more than an electric one. In terms of power, EVs in general have the (13) _____ (fast) acceleration compared with petrol or LPG. Best of all, EVs emit no carbon dioxide or other greenhouse gases, so they are the (14) _____ (harmful) to the environment compared with either petrol or LPG vehicles.

4 Match the sentences with their language functions.

Sentence
1 I'm sorry about the delay.
2 Sorry, could you repeat your surname, please?
3 Is that B-E-N or B-E-N-N?
4 Would you mind sending me the invoice today?
5 I'd like to speak to the manager, please.
6 Would you like me to send you a brochure?

Language function
a) saying what you want
b) offering to do something
c) checking what someone said
d) asking someone to do something
e) checking how to spell something
f) apologising for doing something

5 Complete the phone conversation. Add capital letters where necessary. You don't need all the words in the box.

| I I'll I'd do did will shall would could |

- *MobileExpress. This is Customer Service, Robert speaking. How can I help you?*
- Hello. (1) _____ like some information about your new mobile phone, please.
- *Certainly. (2) _____ you like me to text you some details?*
- Yes, please. Or do you think you (3) _____ send them by email?
- *Of course. (4) _____ I send a PDF?*
- Yes, that's fine.
- *Good. So (5) _____ I have your email address, please?*
- Yes, it's db30@easisoft.com
- *Sorry, (6) _____ you say db13?*
- No, db30.
- *Thanks. And how (7) _____ you spell easisoft?*
- E-A-S-I-S-O-F-T.
- *Right. (8) _____ send it today.*

6 The word *one* is missing from six places in this dialogue. Mark the places.

- *Hello, I'd like to buy an external hard drive, please.*
- Certainly. We have two types. There's with a cable and there's a wireless. There are two types of wireless drives. There's with an SD card slot and there's with no SD slot. Which would you like?
- *I'd like the wireless with the SD card slot, please.*

7 Match these descriptions of a 4 × 4 vehicle.

1 It has a long wheelbase.
2 It has low fuel consumption.
3 It has high clearance.
4 It has strong towing power.
5 It has large fuel capacity.
6 It has good driver visibility.

a) It can drive a long way on one tank of petrol.
b) It can pull another vehicle or trailer easily.
c) The petrol tank is very big.
d) The drive shaft is long.
e) The driver can see clearly all around.
f) There's a lot of space between the ground and the chassis.

8 Change these instructions into a description of a process, using the passive.

> **How to clean a spark plug**
>
> 1 Take off the spark plug cover.
> 2 Loosen the spark plug with a special wrench.
> 3 Remove the spark plug from the socket.
> 4 Clean the spark plug using a wire brush.
> 5 Replace the spark plug in the socket.
> 6 Tighten the spark plug using the wrench.
> 7 Put the cover back on the spark plug.
>
> *Begin: First of all, the spark plug cover is taken off.*
> *Then, the spark plug is ...*

9 Change the second paragraph into a set of instructions, using imperatives.

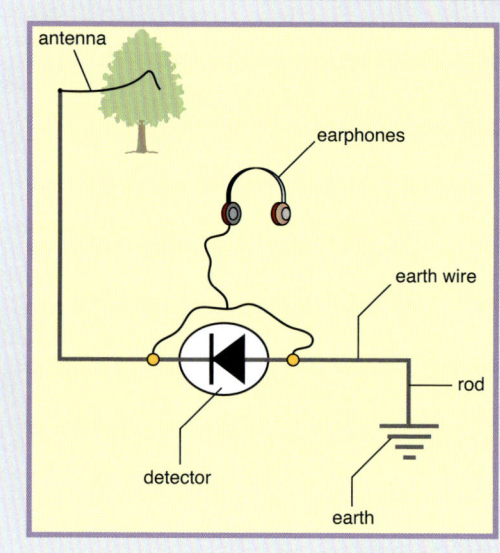

You can make your own radio using a few simple components: two lengths of wire (one 3 m long and the other 6 m long), a metal rod, earphones and a detector. This is how to do it.

First, the rod is hammered into the ground. Then, the insulation is stripped off the end of the 3-metre wire. The wire is twisted around the rod ten times to make a good connection. This is the earth wire. Next, the detector is attached to the other end of the earth wire. The 6-metre wire is now taken and one end is connected to the other end of the detector. (This wire is your antenna.) The antenna is hung from a tree (making sure that the bare end does not touch the earth). The two wires from the earphones are connected to each end of the detector. Finally, the earphones are put on. Now you can hear the radio station (if you are very close to the transmitter!).

Begin: 1 Hammer the rod into the ground.
2 Strip the insulation off the end of the 3-metre wire.

10 Make a set of headings for a talk on these topics. Make each heading begin with a verb ending in **-ing**.

1 First, I'd like to talk about how the communications satellite is launched.
2 After that, I'll talk about how the programmes are transmitted to the satellite.
3 Then, I'll look at how the digital signals are received from the satellite.
4 Next, I'll explain how your satellite dish and digital receiver are installed.
5 Then, I'll go on to mention how your dish is connected to the digital TV receiver.
6 The next topic is how high-frequency signals are converted to low-frequency ones.
7 Then, I'll move on to how the video and audio are extracted from the digital signal.
8 Finally, I'll mention how the video and audio are played via the TV set.
Example: *1 Launching the communications satellite*

11 **Complete these. Use hyphens (-). Note: Be careful with plural nouns.**
1. The plane is ready for the road. It's a <u>road-ready</u> plane.
2. The engine has a cycle of four strokes. It's a <u>4-stroke</u> engine.
3. The propeller has three blades. It's a _____ propeller.
4. The cable is six metres long. It's a _____ cable.
5. This computer is activated when you use your voice. It's a _____ computer.
6. That ticket machine starts when you touch the screen. It's a _____ ticket machine.

12 **Ask and answer questions about a car assembly plant.**

Action

1	deliver car parts	a)	*method*: truck or rail
		b)	*destination*: delivery area
2	carry parts	a)	*destination*: different parts of plant
		b)	*method*: forklift trucks or conveyor belts
3	weld panels to frame	a)	*location*: body shop
		b)	*agent*: 400 robots
		c)	*purpose*: make the body of car
4	check the car body	a)	*time*: after painting
		b)	*agent*: human workers
		c)	*purpose*: look for faults in the paint
5	insert windscreen	a)	*destination*: front of car body
		b)	*agent*: robots
		c)	*method*: laser guides
6	move chassis and body simultaneously	a)	*destination*: final assembly line
		b)	*purpose*: attach body to chassis

location = where something happens
destination = where something is going to

1. a) How are the car parts delivered? They're delivered by truck or rail.
   b) Where are they delivered? To the delivery area.

13 **Write full sentences using the passive.**

Example: *1 The car parts are delivered to the delivery area by truck or rail.*

14 **Rewrite this set of instructions as a paragraph describing a process. Use the passive form of the verbs.**

Servicing a car battery

Open the bonnet of the car. Locate the battery.
Loosen the battery cables, using a wrench. Remove the battery cables from the posts.
Always remove the negative (or earth) cable first, then the positive.
Carefully lay the detached ends of the cables to one side.
Wipe away corrosion from the top of the battery, using baking soda and water.
If corrosion is very heavy, you can clean it from the posts using a wire brush.
Apply petroleum jelly to the inside of the terminals and the posts.
Reattach the cables. Close the car bonnet.

Begin: First the bonnet of the car is opened and the battery is located. Then ...

PROJECT » **15** **Research an industry you are interested in.**

- Find out about an important process in the industry.
- Draw a flow chart of the main stages in the process.
- Write a description of the process.
- Explain the process to the class.

5 Descriptions

1 Uses

START HERE » 1 Think of some tools or devices you use. Discuss why they are useful.

READING » 2 Read the descriptions 1–3 and match them with the objects A and B. Which item is not shown?

1 What do you do if your electric car runs out of charge on the open road a few kilometres before you reach the next charging station? The SparkCharge Roadie allows you to charge your car on the roadside. It's portable and it's designed to give you around eight kilometres of driving after five minutes of charging.

2 This is designed to jump, dive, roll and move over and under water at 80 km/h on the surface and 40 km/h under water. The watercraft is a two-seat, five-metre long, underwater vehicle, shaped like a dolphin. It acts as a jetski and as a fast submersible.

3 Have you forgotten where you put your keys? Use this smart Bluetooth-enabled device and app to find them. Simply attach the tag to your keys and download the tracking app on your smartphone. Then, if you can't find them later, open the app on your phone and you will be able to see a map that shows the exact location of your keys.

SPEAKING » 3 Discuss the objects in 2 with a partner. What do you think of them? Are they useful for you?

LISTENING » 4 ◆)) 5.1 Listen to these people answering questions about the inventions. Identify the inventions in 2.

a) Invention number _____
b) Invention number _____
c) Invention number _____

5 Listen again and complete the dialogues.

A: So, tell me about this invention. What's it for?
B: It's (1) _____.
A: OK. What about this device? What's it used for?
B: It's (2) _____.
A: Tell me about this invention. What can it be used for?
B: You (3) _____.

LANGUAGE »

Present simple	What does this button do? It stops the machine.
for + verb **-ing**	What's this tool for? It's for hammering in nails. What's this machine used for? It's used for producing drinking water.
to + verb	You use this machine to charge electric cars. This device is designed to find lost objects.
act as + noun	The fan of a hovercraft acts as a propeller.

SPEAKING »

6 Work in pairs. Make questions and answers about the uses of the devices in 2.

A: What's this device used for?
B: It's used for turning nuts and bolts without hurting your hand.

7 What do you think these devices are used for? Discuss them with your partner.

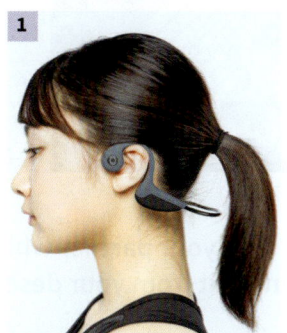

VOCABULARY »

Many nouns end in *-er* or *-or*. These are often *agent nouns*. An agent noun shows the person or thing that does an action, e.g. A *calculator* (n.) is a machine. It *calculates* (vb.) sums.

Note these changes of spelling when you add *-er/-or*:
- double the final consonant after a short vowel. Example: *propel → propeller*
- delete the final *-e*. Example: *receive → receiver*

8 Find the agent nouns for the verbs in the box. Use a dictionary if necessary.

calculate   conduct   contain   generate   receive   stabilise   transmit

9 Fill in the blanks. Use nouns from your answers in 8.

1 The number pad on a computer can be used as a _____ .
2 Your body can act as a _____ of electricity in a thunderstorm.
3 A car engine functions as a _____ when it recharges the battery.
4 At least one of the antennas inside a smartphone operates as a _____ and as a _____ of radio signals.

TASK »

10 Work in small groups. Choose one of these objects with your group.

a tin can, a belt, a brick, a tyre, a water pipe

- Brainstorm as many unusual uses for them as you can.
- Write down your best ideas.
- Present your group's best ideas to the class.

Examples: *A tin can* – You can use it to store pencils. You can put flowers in it. You can use it as a cup. Two or three cans together can act as a door bell, etc.

2 Appearance

START HERE » 1 Do you know where these buildings are?

(Answers on page 115)

2 Choose one of the buildings. Don't tell your partner which one. Describe its appearance. Can your partner identify it from your description?

READING » 3 Read these notes. Match the buildings (A–D) with the descriptions.

1 This building looks like a huge ship, an ocean liner, sailing up the river. One part of the building is shaped like three hulls. The other part looks like the decks and the bridge.

2 The building looks like a TV transmitter. It has three spherical structures. The bottom two are connected by a structure which is shaped like a ladder. It looks like three onions on a skewer! The foot of the building has legs, like a tripod.

3 The skyscraper is shaped like a giant sail. The sail is standing on a short surfboard in the sea.

4 This building has three parts. In the centre there's a tall H-shaped building. On the left there's the top part of a dome, like an upside-down plate. On the right there's the bottom part of a dome, like a soup bowl.

5 It consists of three L-shaped structures, attached to each other. It looks like a square link in a chain.

LANGUAGE » You can describe the *shape* or *appearance* of something in these ways:
- The building **looks like** a TV transmitter.
- The building **is shaped like** a dome. It's a dome-**shaped** building.
- The plan is **in the shape of** an L. It's an L-**shaped** plan.
- The screen is **in the shape of a circle**. It's a **circular** screen.

4 One description in 3 has no photo. Draw the building. Do you know where it is?

38 5 Descriptions

VOCABULARY »

5 Match the nouns to the shapes.

circle cone cube cylinder hemisphere rectangle
semicircle sphere square triangle

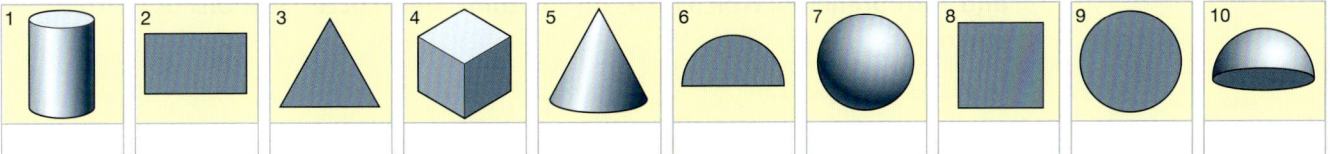

6 Write an adjective for each noun.

Example: *cylinder – cylindrical*

7 Underline the stressed syllable in each word.

1 tri ang le
2 rect ang u lar
3 cir cu lar
4 cy lin der
5 tri ang u lar
6 circ le
7 rect ang le
8 cy lind ric al

8 🔊 5.2 Listen and check your answers to 7.

9 Underline the correct words.

1 A surfboard sail is roughly *triangle/triangular* in shape, with one curved side.
2 A food tin (or can) is basically a metal *cylinder/cylindrical*.
3 TVs and computers normally have *rectangle/rectangular* screens.
4 Don't cut that wood with the hand saw. It's quicker to use the *circle/circular* saw.
5 My bass amplifier is the new *cube/cubic* model. It's exactly 30 × 30 × 30 cm.
6 The Earth is not a perfect *sphere/spherical*. It is flatter at the poles.
7 The spaceship's re-entry capsule is in the shape of a *cone/conical*.
8 A protractor is a *semi-circle/semi-circular* instrument for measuring angles.

10 Match the names of the objects in the box with their pictures.

A-frame E-clip G-clamp G-clip T-junction U-bend U-bolt V-engine

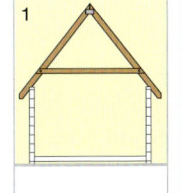 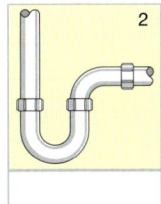 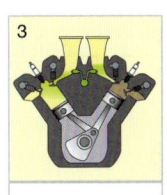   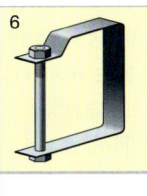 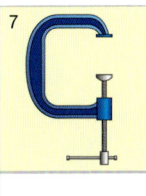 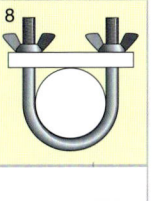

TASK »

11 Work in pairs, A and B. Play *twenty questions*.

Student A: Think of an everyday object. It could be a vehicle, a tool, a measuring instrument or a useful device. Don't tell your partner what it is. Answer your partner's questions.

Student B: Ask a maximum of 20 questions and try to guess Student A's object. You can't ask directly *What is it?* But you can ask questions such as these:

- **appearance:** *What does it look like? What colour is it? What shape is it?*
- **use:** *What's it for? What's it used for? What does it do?*
- **materials:** *What's it made of?*
- **dimensions:** *How long is it? How wide is it?*
- **properties:** *Is it flexible? Is it water-resistant?*

When you have finished, change roles.

3 Definitions

START HERE »

1 Here are some ideas for devices that appeared on a TV programme for inventors and entrepreneurs. Which ideas do you think were successful? Discuss with a partner.

(Answers on page 113)

- Are you a technical entrepreneur?
- Do you have a good idea for inventing and manufacturing a new device?
- Do you think you can sell your device and make a profit?
- Do you need money to start your business?

Explain your idea to a team of rich business experts – the Dragons. Try to persuade them to invest their money in your idea. Here are some ideas from previous programmes:

1. An electronic device for boiling eggs without using water.
2. A boat alarm system for finding an MOB (man overboard).
3. A do-it-yourself kit for repairing a smartphone that has fallen into some water.
4. A seat-belt adjuster for protecting children in car booster seats.

LISTENING »

2 🔊 5.3 Listen to the questions and answers about the inventions in 1. Complete the sentences with *which*, *that* or *who*.

1. This invention is an electronic device (1) _____ can boil eggs without using water.
2. LifeGuard is an alarm system (2) _____ can find someone (3) _____ has fallen off a boat.
3. This is a do-it-yourself kit (4) _____ enables you to repair your smartphone if it has fallen into some water.
4. It's a seat-belt adjuster (5) _____ protects children in car booster seats.

LANGUAGE »

Word	be	Type	Defining relative clause	
			Pronoun	Function
LifeGuard	is	an alarm system	which	can find an MOB.
ReviveAPhone	is	equipment	that	repairs smartphones.
Inventors	are	people	who	create new devices.

- *which* is used with things
- *that* can replace *which* or *who*
- *who* is used with people

VOCABULARY »

3 Fill in the blanks with the most suitable 'type' noun in the box.

| device instrument system technician tool vehicle |

1 A solar panel is a/an _____. It converts sunlight into electricity.
2 The hovercraft is a/an _____. It carries people over land and sea.
3 A lab assistant is a/an _____. He/She maintains the equipment in a laboratory.
4 A torque wrench is a/an _____. It tightens nuts and bolts.
5 GPS is a satellite _____. It gives the location of objects on the ground.
6 An ammeter is a/an _____. It measures electric current.

4 Combine each pair of sentences in 3 into a single sentence in the form of a definition. Use *which*, *that* or *who*.

Example: *1 A solar panel is a device which converts sunlight into electricity.*

READING »

5 Read this advertisement and answer the questions below.

Alarm pods

Hydrophone

Display

This digital-sonar alarm system transmits a signal to your boat crew if you fall overboard into the water. It consists of three devices: the alarm pod, the hydrophone and the display.

The alarm pod is an egg-shaped device, worn by each crew member, which transmits a digital-sonar coded signal when it is submerged in water.

The hydrophone is a transducer, attached to the inside of the boat hull, that listens for signals from the alarm pod.

The display is a control unit, attached to the dashboard of the boat, which shows information from the hydrophone by means of LEDs and digital displays.

When the man overboard (MOB) hits the water, the alarm pod is submerged. The alarm pod has two pins. If these pins are in contact with water for one second and the contact is constant across the two pins, the pod is activated. It then sends a signal under the water. This signal is picked up by the hydrophone, which relays it to the display.

Four things then happen immediately:
- Bright LEDs in the display show a visible alarm.
- Speakers on the boat sound an audible alarm.
- The MOB's location is shown on the display via the internal GPS system.
- Red and green LEDs navigate the boat to the MOB's location.

1 Which device acts as (a) the transmitter (b) the receiver (c) the controller?
2 Which device is fixed (a) inside the hull (b) on the crew's body (c) on the deck?
3 What happens if drops of rain fall on the pins on the alarm pod? Does the alarm sound? Why/Why not?
4 Does the signal travel from the pod to the display unit (a) directly (b) via the hydrophone (c) via GPS (satellite)?
5 Which word in the text means (a) able to be seen (b) able to be heard?

TASK »

6 Work in small groups. Decide on an idea for a new invention. In a single sentence, give the definition of your device. Then, in a few sentences, explain how it works.

5 Descriptions

6 Procedures

1 Safety

START HERE   **1** Make a list of the hazards (A–H) in this warehouse in note form.

READING   **2** Read this warehouse safety poster. Match the rules to the hazards in 1.

Warehouse safety

1. Hand trucks must not be overloaded.
2. Aisles have to be kept free of all blockages.
3. Boxes need to be pushed in until they are level with the edge of the shelf.
4. Gas cylinders must always be strapped or chained to hand trucks.
5. The forks of a forklift truck must never be used for carrying people.
6. Larger boxes should not be stacked on higher shelves.
7. Trucks must be pulled, not pushed, up a ramp.
8. Only one item should be removed from a shelf at one time.

LANGUAGE

Helmets	must/should/have to/need to	be	worn here.
	must/should	not be	taken off.

3 Where can you see these labels? What do they mean?

4 What could be inside containers with the labels?

> bottles of liquid   fruit   food   glass   hats   electrical goods   plants

5 Complete these explanations of the labels. Use the correct form of the modals and the passive form of the verbs in brackets.

1. This item _____ (need/handle) carefully.
   It _____ (must not/drop or throw).
2. This item _____ (need/carry) this way up.
   It _____ (must not/turn) upside down.
3. This item _____ (should/keep) inside the warehouse.
   It _____ (have/protect) from the rain.
4. This box _____ (should/deliver) as soon as possible.
   It _____ (must not/leave) for more than three days.
5. This box _____ (have/freeze).
   It _____ (must not/leave) outside the freezer.

Example: *1 This item needs to be handled carefully. It must not be …*

6 Change the instructions in 5 into the active form.

Example: *1 You need to handle this item carefully. You mustn't …*

TASK » 7 Three safety procedures have become mixed up. Work in pairs, A and B. Put all the notes together under the best headings in the best order. Each procedure has eight steps.

Student A: Turn to page 112 to find your set of notes.
Student B: Use the notes below.

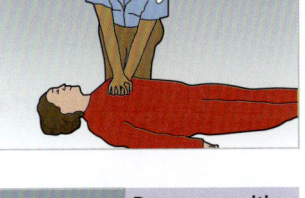
CPR

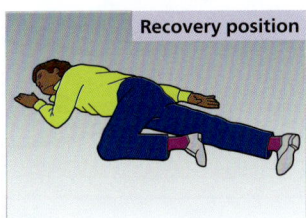
Recovery position

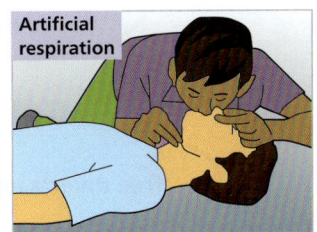
Artificial respiration

FIRST AID AFTER ELECTRIC SHOCK

CHEMICAL SPILL PROCEDURE

FIRE EVACUATION PROCEDURE

If you hear an alarm, remain calm.

Do not return to the building unless you are authorised by the fire department.

Check the person's condition.

If there is no pulse, give the person CPR.

If the person is breathing, they should be placed in the recovery position.

Do not stop to collect your belongings.

Remain near workroom until Chemical Safety staff arrives.

Stop work.

The workroom must be secured to keep others out.

Move at least 30 metres from building.

Attend to any injured persons if you can do so safely.

Call 112.

6 Procedures 43

2 Emergency

START HERE »

1 Work in small groups. Decide on a plan to rescue the diver.

> Mike, Ben and Tom are scuba divers. They go in their motorboat about 2 km from land and drop anchor. Mike and Ben dive down to a shipwreck on the seabed. Tom stays on the boat. As Ben and Mike return to their boat, Mike has an accident, and injures his leg. His leg is trapped in the shipwreck and he can't move. Ben sees that Mike has a problem so he swims back down to help him.

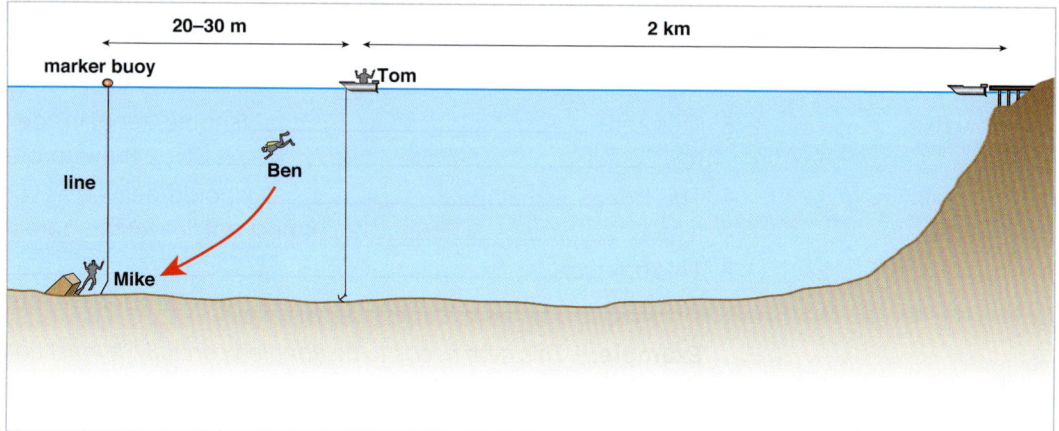

In your group:
- brainstorm and make a list of all the tasks Ben has to do, in any order
- discuss and decide on the best order to do the tasks

LISTENING »

2 🔊 6.1 Listen to this diving instructor brainstorming with trainees how to rescue someone trapped under water. Number the points in the order in which they are mentioned.

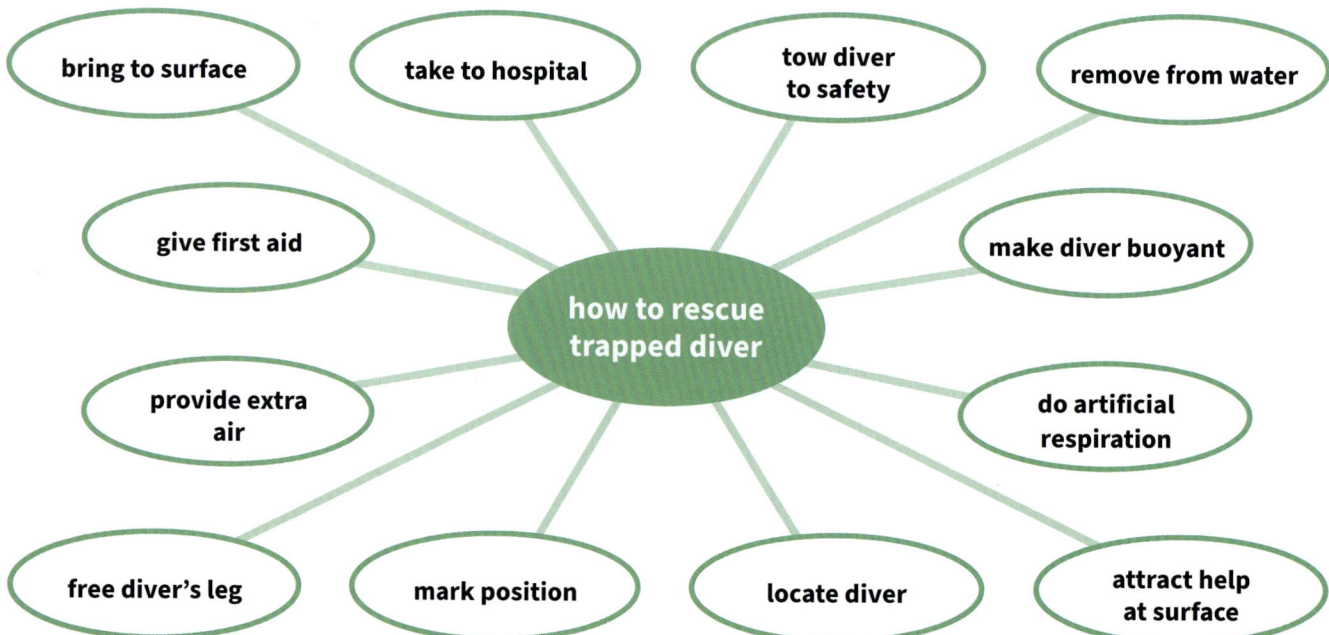

44 6 Procedures

3 🔊 6.2 Now the instructor is getting the trainees to put their ideas into the best order. Listen and number these notes in the correct order.

• Diver's air supply low?	→	Give extra gas cylinder to diver.
• Diver's location under water unknown?	→	Locate diver and mark their position. 1
• Diver not buoyant at the surface?	→	Inflate diver's jacket.
• Not breathing?	→	Give artificial respiration.
• Other boats in area?	→	Send signal for help.
• Serious injury?	→	Call helicopter to take to hospital.
• Diver close to boat or land?	→	Remove from water.
• No help available at surface?	→	Tow diver to boat or land.
• Diver trapped underwater?	→	Free diver with knife.
• Diver submerged in water?	→	Bring to surface carefully.
• Diver needs immediate treatment?	→	Give first aid.

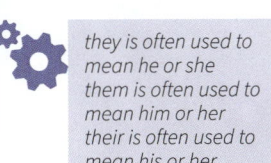

they is often used to mean *he* or *she*
them is often used to mean *him* or *her*
their is often used to mean *his* or *her*

SPEAKING »

4 Make full questions and answers based on 3.

A: *What should we do if the diver's location under water is unknown?*
B: *You should locate them and mark their position.*

LANGUAGE »

Must is used to show that an action is necessary, e.g. *Safety helmets must be worn at all times.*

Should is used to show that you're **recommending** or **suggesting** an action, e.g. *People think safety helmets should be orange. In my opinion, they should be yellow.*

Should + passive is used in the **recommendations** section of a report, e.g. *New first aid equipment should be purchased immediately.*

READING »

5 Read this email. Which section gives:

- *old information* (= what Rosy already knows)?
- *new information* (= what Rosy needs to know)?
- *action* (= what Rosy needs to do)?

From: Rescue Centre Manager
To: Air-Sea Rescue Operations Co-ordinator
Subject: This morning's rescue operation

Hi Rosy

You'll remember that we talked about the trapped diver (Mike) on the phone this morning. The rescue leader has just told me that Mike is now going to the hospital by helicopter. I'm holding a meeting next week to discuss our rescue procedures. Could you please send me your recommendations for improving them?

Regards, Don

WRITING »

6 Write an email giving Rosy's reply. Give old information, new information and action. Include six recommendations in the new information.

Choose six items from the table in 3, or give some of your own ideas for recommendations.

3 Directions

START HERE »

1 Identify these landmarks on the photo.

> flyover   gantry   motorway
> roundabout   slip road   underpass

READING »

2 Match the directions with the maps.

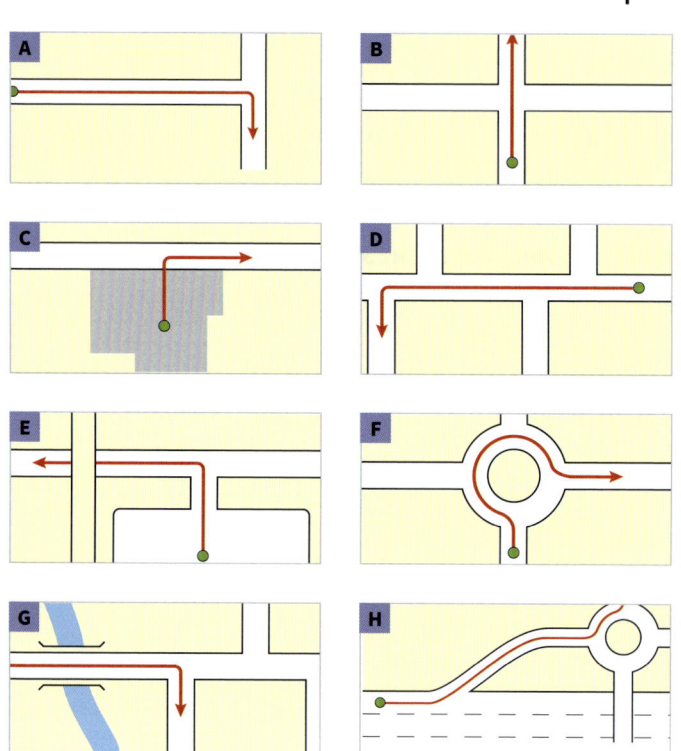

1 take the second turning on the left
2 take the third exit from the roundabout
3 turn right at the T-junction
4 come out of the building and turn right
5 go straight ahead at the crossroads
6 leave the motorway by the slip road and turn left at the roundabout
7 go over the bridge and take the first road on the right
8 come out of the car park and turn left under the flyover

LANGUAGE »

First describe the situation …	then give the instruction
There is a STOP sign at the end of the road.	Turn left here.
There are two sets of traffic lights on this road.	Turn right at the second set.
When you come out of the station,	turn right into Market Street.
You'll see a police station on your left.	Don't turn left here. Take the second turning on the left.
If you cross a bridge over the river, you've gone too far.	Do a U-turn. Go back across the bridge. Then take the first turning on the right.

46   6 Procedures

READING » 3 Read this email and mark TurboTech on the map.

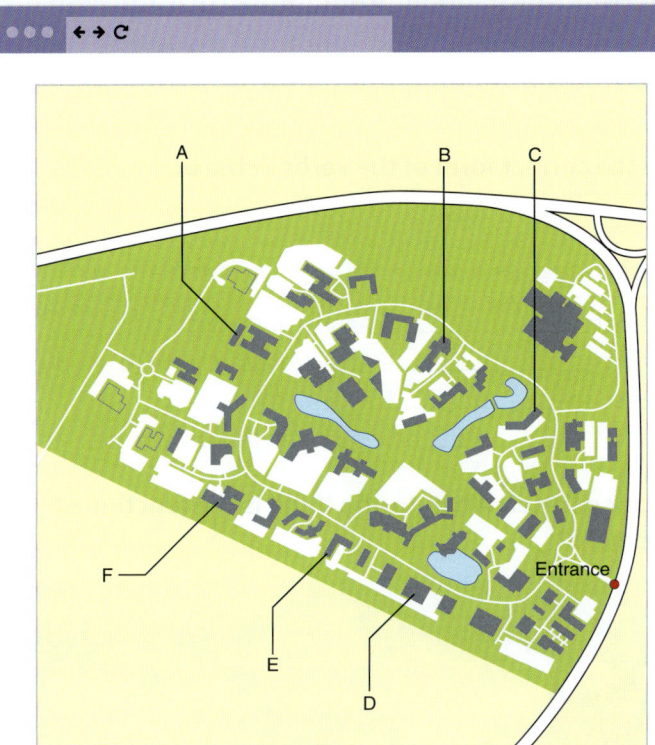

Dear Ms Olsen

Thank you for your email yesterday requesting directions to TurboTech. It's located in the Science Park in Cambridge.

After you enter the Science Park, you'll come to a roundabout. At the roundabout, take the second exit (we drive on the left in the UK!). Then go straight ahead. You'll pass a lake on your left. After the lake, you'll see the TurboTech sign. Take the first road on your left, and TurboTech is on your right. Drive into the car park and then walk to the Reception Desk.

I look forward to meeting you and your colleague tomorrow at 11.

Ibrahim Anders, General Manager

LISTENING » 4 🔊 6.3 Listen to these telephone directions and mark the Engineering Department and the Sports Centre on the map.

Note: the university is in a country which drives on the left.

SPEAKING » 5 Work in pairs, A and B. Give each other telephone directions to places on the map in 4.

Student A: Turn to page 112.

Student B: Turn to page 114.

TASK » 6 Work in pairs. List three local places you know.

- Tell your partner how to get there.
- Listen to your partner's directions and draw sketch maps.
- Exchange maps with your partner and check the details.

6 Procedures   47

Review Unit C

1 Complete the sentences. Use the correct form of the verbs in the box.

| carry   convert   detect   start   treat |

1 Jump leads are used for _____ a car with a flat battery.
2 The purpose of a hydrophone is to _____ signals under water.
3 The function of a transducer is to _____ energy from one form to another.
4 A first aid kit should only be used for _____ minor injuries.
5 A forklift truck must be used to _____ boxes around the warehouse.

2 Work in pairs. Discuss with your partner. What do you think is the function of each item of the diver's equipment?

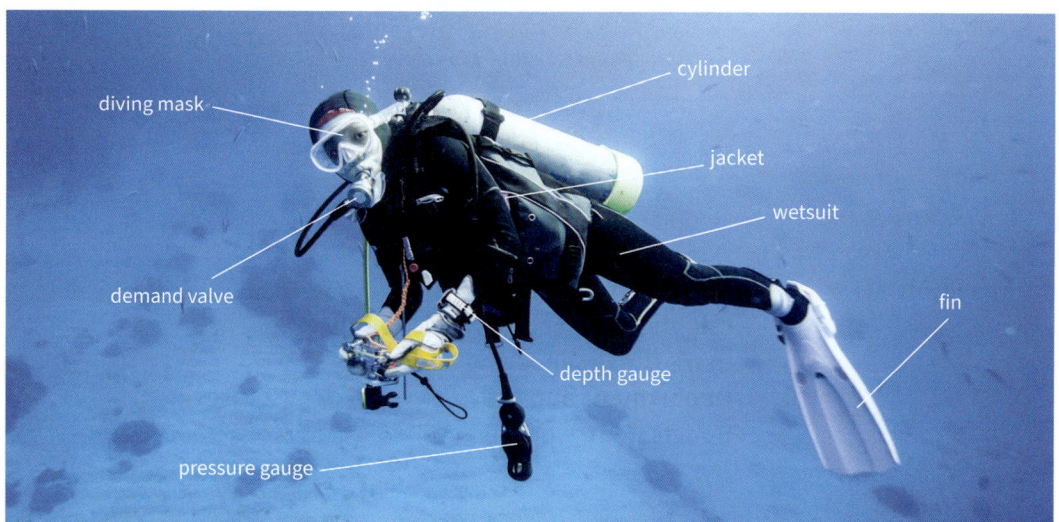

3 Take turns with your partner to describe the function of each item of equipment. Use the correct form of the verbs.

Equipment	Function	
1 demand valve	control the flow of air to the diver	(for)
2 cylinder	transport air under high pressure	(used to)
3 pressure gauge	indicate the amount of compressed air in the cylinder	(present simple)
4 fins	propel the diver through the water	(used for)
5 depth gauge	indicate the depth of the water	(designed to)
6 wetsuit	keep the diver warm	(for)
7 diving mask	allow diver to see clearly under water	(designed to)
8 pressure gauge	a warning for the diver	(act as)
9 demand valve	supply compressed air to the diver	(present simple)
10 jacket	make the diver buoyant	(used for)

Example: *1 The demand valve is for controlling the flow of air to the diver.*

4 Supply the questions in this interview about the Man Overboard alarm system on page 41.

- *So tell us about your invention. What's (1) _____?*
- It's called a 'digital-sonar alarm system' for boats.
- *What's (2) _____?*
- Well, it's for finding people when they fall off a boat into the water.
- *I see. How (3) _____?*
- Well, when the person falls into the water, a sensor on the pod sends a sonar signal to the hydrophone.
- *Hold on a minute. What exactly (4) _____?*
- A hydrophone is a transducer which can detect signals under water.
- *I see. So who (5) _____ for?*
- It's designed for everyone on the boat. The crew and their family.
- *OK, so tell me about the pod. What shape (6) _____?*
- Well, it's shaped a bit like an egg.
- *How (7) _____?*
- It's quite small. It's about 15 cm long.
- *Where (8) _____?*
- You wear it on your belt. It has a clip.
- *What (9) _____?*
- It's made of a very tough polymer.
- *What (10) _____?*
- It's a very bright colour, usually yellow or red.

5 What do you think these are for? Discuss with a partner.

6 Write a description of the four items in 5. Describe (a) their appearance and (b) their function. What is their purpose? (Answers on page 115.)

7 Make definitions.

1 a webcam	instrument	loosen and tighten nuts on wheels
2 fibreglass	system	repair underwater pipes and machines
3 artificial respiration	tool	powered by electricity from a solar panel
4 GPS	technician	feeds live images or videos through a
5 a sub-sea mechanic	vehicle	computer network
6 a solar-powered car	procedure	use satellites to locate your position
7 a wheel wrench	device	calculate diver's depth in the water
8 a depth gauge	material	used for making hulls of boats
		help a casualty to breathe

Example: *1 A webcam is a device which feeds live images or videos through a computer network.*

8 Write a reply to this email.
Note: the campus is in a country which drives on the right.

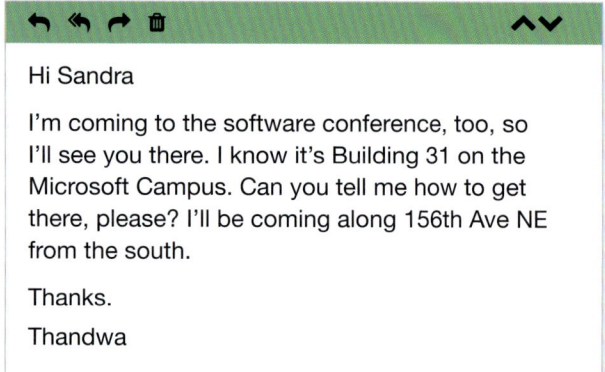

Hi Sandra

I'm coming to the software conference, too, so I'll see you there. I know it's Building 31 on the Microsoft Campus. Can you tell me how to get there, please? I'll be coming along 156th Ave NE from the south.

Thanks.

Thandwa

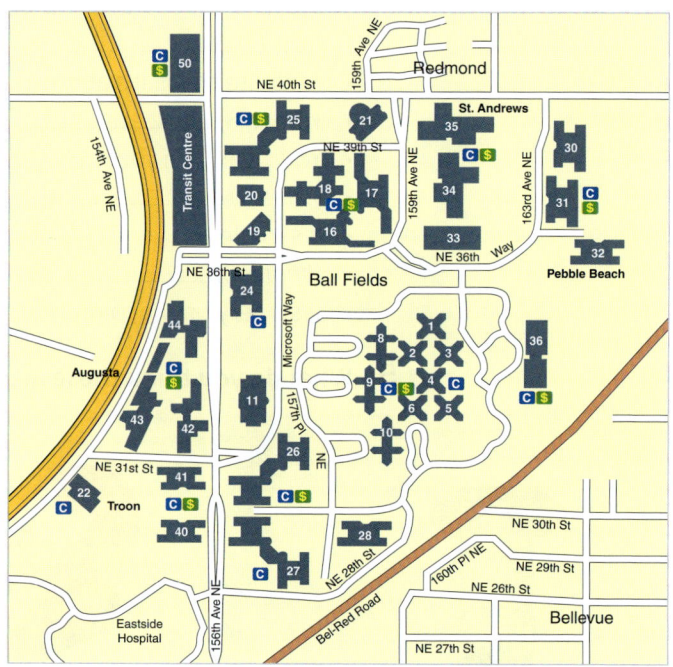

9 Change these instructions into the passive.

1 You must carry two air cylinders at all times during a dive.

2 All staff have to wear lifejackets on board this oil rig.

3 You must not stack boxes or crates in the aisles.

4 You need to freeze all this food before you send it to the warehouse.

5 Workers should never use forklift trucks as people carriers.

6 You have to push trucks down a ramp. You must never pull them down.

Example: *1 Two air cylinders must be carried at all times during a dive.*

10 Work in pairs, A and B.

   Student A
   1 Turn to page 112. Describe the object and ask Student B to draw it. Then check B's drawing. Does it look like your object?
   2 Listen to Student B's description of an object and draw it from their description. Show your drawing to B.

   Student B
   1 Listen to Student A's description of an object and draw it from their description. Show your drawing to A.
   2 Turn to page 115. Describe your object and ask Student A to draw it. Then check A's drawing. Does it look like your object?

11 **Work in pairs. Discuss these questions about the fire extinguisher. Make notes of your answers.**

   - This device should NOT be used to put out electrical fires? Why not?
   - What are (a) the cylinder and (b) the siphon made of?
   - What properties do these materials have? Why are these properties important here?
   - What function(s) does the valve have?
   - What is the purpose of the rod? Why does it have a sharp point?
   - How do you activate the extinguisher?
   - What happens when you activate it? How does it work?
   - What forces the water to rise up the siphon?
   - How do you think you should hold and move the extinguisher when you are fighting a fire?
   - What safety rules do you think you need when using a fire extinguisher?

12 **With your partner, produce a safety poster about this type of extinguisher. Use your notes and add any other information you know.**

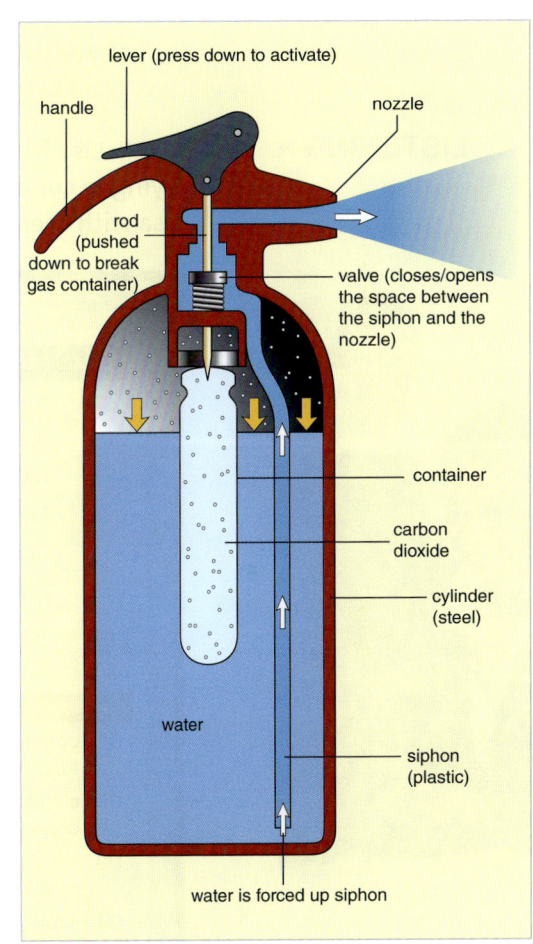

PROJECT » 13 **Find out about an important device or piece of equipment used in your technical field.**

   - Note down the key information.
   - Prepare a short talk.
   - Describe the device or equipment to the class.

7 Services

1 Technical support

START HERE »

1 What problems have you had with computers? What were your solutions?

2 Work with a partner. Decide on the best solutions to these computer problems.

1 You can't log into your company network from home. Your password is rejected.
2 The image on your monitor is too large and you can't see the whole page.
3 You can open your incoming emails, but you can't open their attachments.
4 A website says **CLICK HERE TO SEE PHOTO**. You click, but nothing happens.
5 You can't get a wireless connection between your computer and your router.
6 Now you have the wireless connection between your computer and your router, but you can't access the internet. A message says **LIMITED OR NO CONNECTIVITY**.

LISTENING »

3 🔊 7.1 Lisa is an IT support technician in a large company. Her colleagues are trying to connect their home computers to the company network. They phone Lisa with their problems. Listen and complete Lisa's report.

CALL	PROBLEM	DIAGNOSIS	SOLUTION
1	Network rejects password	D3	S2
2	Can't see full page on screen; icons too large		
3	Can't open email attachments		
4	Click on link, but photo doesn't appear		
5	Can't connect computer wirelessly with router		
6	Can't access internet through wireless connection		

DIAGNOSIS CODE	
D1	computer has different IP address from router
D2	electronic devices interfere with connection
D3	network system remembers wrong password
D4	wrong screen resolution settings
D5	firewall blocks pop-ups
D6	security level in email program is too high

SOLUTION CODE	
S1	reboot the router and computer
S2	uncheck the remember password box
S3	increase the screen resolution to correct setting
S4	switch off block pop-up adverts in firewall
S5	move the router to a different location
S6	lower the security level for attachments

4 🔊 7.2 Listen to how Lisa diagnoses the problem. Complete the statements with the verbs in the box.

| could   may   might   must |

1 You _____ have checked the **REMEMBER PASSWORD** box.
2 Your computer _____ be using the wrong screen resolution settings.
3 Your email program _____ be blocking the attachments.
4 Your firewall _____ be blocking the pop-ups.
5 Another electronic device _____ be interfering with the connection.
6 You _____ have given the computer a different IP address from the router.

5 Which statements in 4 show that Lisa thinks her diagnosis is
- certainly correct? Write *C* after the statement.
- possibly correct? Write *P* after the statement.

6 🔊 7.3 Listen to how Lisa suggests a solution. Complete the statements. Use the correct form of the verbs in the box.

| could   don't   lower   suggest   try   type |

1 Now try _____ in the correct password.
2 Try _____ your security level.
3 Well, you _____ move the phone away. Or why _____ you move the router around?
4 I _____ you _____ moving the router to a different location.

LANGUAGE »

Diagnosing a problem
- present possibility: *may/might/could* + *be*/present continuous, e.g. *The file may/might/could be too large.*
- present certainty: *must* + *be*/present continuous, e.g. *The firewall must be blocking the attachments.*
- past possibility: *must/may/might* + present perfect, e.g. *You may/might have broken it.*
- past certainty: *must* + present perfect, e.g. *You must have broken it.*

Suggesting a solution
- *try* + verb + *-ing*. *Try clicking on the 'undo' button.*
- *Why don't you …? Why don't you click on the 'undo' button?*
- *could. You could click on the 'undo' button.*

7 Rephrase these. Use language from above.

1 *Diagnosis*: your switch is probably broken. *Suggestion*: change it
2 *D*: it's possible your cable is loose. *S*: push it firmly into the socket
3 *D*: you are definitely using the wrong IP address *S*: reboot the router
4 *D*: perhaps the program has frozen *S*: press CTRL-ALT-DEL
5 *D*: the mouse has definitely stopped working *S*: disconnect and reconnect
6 *D*: it's certain your file is too large for the disk *S*: compress it

Example: *1 Your switch might be broken. Try changing it.*

7 Services

2 Reporting to clients

START HERE »

1. How can architects make tall buildings safer in fires or other emergencies? Brainstorm some ideas in groups.

TASK »

2. Discuss these ideas for safer skyscrapers with your group.
   - Discuss the purpose of the ideas on the diagram.
   - Draw up and complete a table like this.

Ideas for making skyscrapers safer in fires and emergencies	
Idea	Purpose
(a) CCTV cameras	to check everyone's location; to allow controllers to monitor the situation
(b) parachutes	to allow people to escape quickly from the top floors

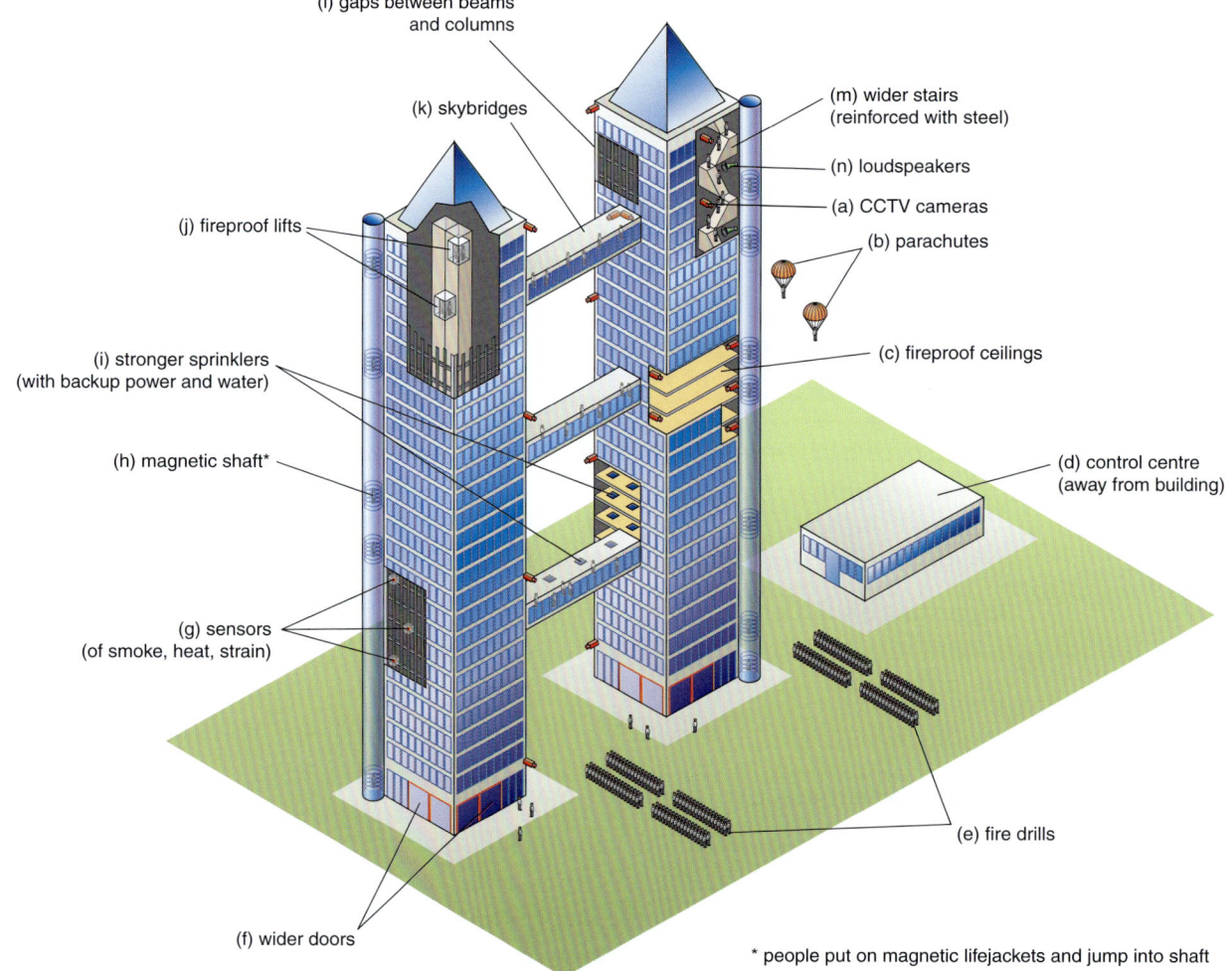

* people put on magnetic lifejackets and jump into shaft

3. Discuss these questions with your group and add notes to your table in 2.
   - Which safety features will work?
   - Which ones will not work, or be too difficult to install?
   - Discuss the reasons.

4. Present your group's decisions to the class.

READING »

5 Read this covering letter and answer the questions below.

1. Who is (a) the client (b) the contractor?
2. What did the client ask the contractor to do and when did he ask it?
3. What has the contractor done?
4. Where is the contractor's report?
5. What does the contractor ask the client to do?
6. Which words introduce good news?

> Mr John Hu
> Director
> Hu Constructions Pte Ltd
>
> Dear Mr Hu
> Safety upgrading of Hu Building
> Thank you for your letter of 24th January authorising us to do the above work.
> I am pleased to inform you that the work was completed last month. Our report is attached. Please let me know if you need clarification of any of the points in the report.
> Yours sincerely
>
> Pierre Van Ek
> Director
> enc. *Report on Safety Modifications to Hu Building.*

Commas are optional:
Dear Mr Hu,
Yours sincerely,

6 Read the contractor's report. Write a letter from the diagram in 2 next to each job report.

SUMMARY REPORT FROM SAFETY DESIGNS LTD

THE FOLLOWING JOBS WERE CARRIED OUT IN THE HU BUILDING DURING JANUARY–OCTOBER:

1. Three walkways were built between the towers to allow people to cross over. (_____)
2. The width of stairs was increased by 25 cm to allow more people to use them. (_____)
3. Fire-resistant material was placed between floors to stop fires from spreading. (_____)
4. Exits on the ground floor were widened by 1 m to allow people to escape more easily. (_____)
5. Elevators were covered with fire-resistant material to protect them. (_____)
6. Structural beams were shortened by 8 cm to allow them to expand in a fire. (_____)
7. Smoke detectors were installed to give early warning of fire. (_____)
8. No equipment for jumping was provided since we decided it was impractical. (_____)

7 Underline examples of the passive in the summary report in 6.

Example: *1 Three walkways <u>were built</u> between the towers …*

LANGUAGE »

| The building work | was | completed | last month. |
| Three walkways | were | built | between the towers. |

8 Change the sentences in the report in 6 into the active.

Example: *1 We built three walkways between the towers to allow people to cross over.*

SPEAKING »

9 Refer to the table your group completed in 2. In your group, roleplay a meeting between client and contractor.

Appoint one member of your group to be the client, John Hu. The other group members are a team of contractors working for Safety Designs Ltd. The contractors have now carried out the work they specified in the table in 2.

In the meeting, the client asks the contractors what changes they made to the building, why they made/did not make the changes and other questions about dimensions, materials, etc. The contractors answer the client's questions.

7 Services 55

3 Dealing with complaints

START HERE »

1 What are the most common customer complaints in your technical field?

2 How should staff deal with a complaint from a customer? Make some guidelines for staff (in note form).

LISTENING »

3 🔊 7.4 Listen to this phone call from a customer with a complaint. Note down the details in the complaints form.

Date and time of call	16/03 10.45
Name of customer	
Order number	
Description of goods	
Model number	
Details of complaint	
Solution offered	☐ replace ☐ repair ☐ refund ☐ reduce
Customer response	☐ accept ☐ reject

4 Listen again to the phone call. Look at the company handbook below. Which procedures are (a) *followed* (b) *broken* by the staff?

Procedure for dealing with a telephone complaint from a customer

1 be friendly, polite and helpful
2 listen carefully
3 show sympathy with the customer's problem but don't admit the company's fault
4 summarise what the customer has told you and check that you have understood correctly
5 record the details and collect the evidence (e.g. receipts or damaged goods)
6 offer a solution (*repair* the item, *replace* it, *refund* the money or *reduce* the price of the next purchase)

TASK »

5 Work in pairs, A and B. Roleplay a phone call between service staff and a customer with a complaint. Before you start, study the audio script of the phone call in 3 on page 124.

Student A: You're the customer. Make notes about your device and what is wrong with it. Include a model name, number and an order number. Then call customer services.

Student B: You work in customer service. Draw up a customer complaints form such as the one in 3. Then take the call from the customer and deal with their complaint.

6 Describe the damage to the suitcase. You do not need all the words in the box.

| broken | burnt | cracked | crushed | dented | split | torn | twisted |

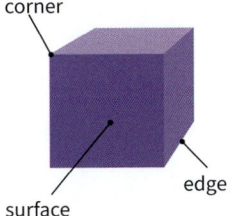

READING »

7 Read this reply to a customer's email of complaint and answer the questions.

Dear Mr Bianchi

Thank you for your email complaining about the robot vacuum you bought from our store. I was sorry to hear that the top surface of the machine was scratched and the edge was cracked.

Unfortunately, we do not have any more robot vacuums in stock at the moment. However, I am pleased to inform you that we will give you your money back in full. In addition, as a gesture of goodwill, we will give you a 10% discount off your next purchase from our store.

I would like to apologise for the inconvenience you have experienced. Please do not hesitate to contact me if you have any further queries.

Yours sincerely

Roberta Wilson

Store Manager

---

1 What did the customer complain about?
2 What does the writer offer to do?
3 Which words (a) show sympathy (b) give an apology?
4 Which words introduce (a) good news (b) bad news?

WRITING »

8 You are the Manager of IT Online Ltd. Reply to this email.

To the Manager, IT Online Ltd

Dear Sir or Madam
I wish to complain about the Mace notebook computer which I ordered from your online store last month (order number 60335/01). The computer was delivered only yesterday. When I opened the box, the adapter was missing. This is very poor service indeed. I look forward to hearing from you.

Peter Bradwell

---

7 Services

8 Energy

1 Wave power

START HERE »

1 Brainstorm in small groups. Make notes or draw simple diagrams.

How can the energy of sea waves be converted into electrical power?

TASK »

2 Study this diagram. It shows one method of converting wave energy into electrical power. With your group
- decide how it works
- explain your group's ideas to the rest of the class.

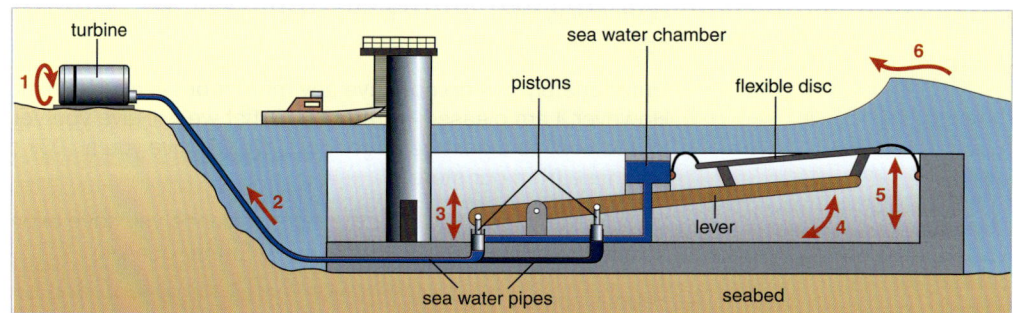

VOCABULARY »

3 Complete this text with the correct motion words.

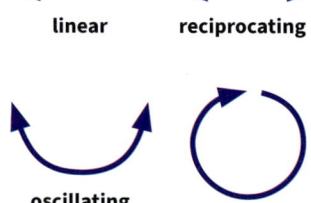

There are four basic motions. First, there is (1) _____ motion. This is movement in a straight line and in one direction. Secondly, there is (2) _____ motion, which is two-way movement backwards and forwards, or up and down (like a piston) in a straight line. The third type is (3) _____ motion, which swings from side to side (like a pendulum). Finally, there is (4) _____ motion, which is motion in a circular direction, like the shaft of a wind turbine.

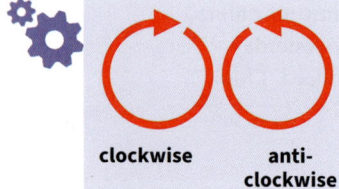

4 Match the numbered arrows in the diagram in 2 with the motion words in 3.

5 Complete these sentences. Use the present simple of the verbs in the box.

1 Propeller shafts _____.
2 A car engine piston _____.
3 Pendulums _____.
4 When you tighten a screw, it _____ clockwise.

| oscillate   reciprocate |
| rotate |

SCANNING » 6 Practise your speed reading. Look for the information you need on the SPEED SEARCH pages (118–119). Try to be the first to complete the task.

Task: Find out five advantages (or benefits) of the wave energy converter.

LISTENING » 7 🔊 8.1 Listen to this presentation about the Wave Energy Converter and complete the listener's notes.

WAVE ENERGY CONVERTER

DEFINITION: system for converting (1)_____ from sea waves into electrical power
LOCATION: fixed to the (2)_____
MAIN COMPONENTS: a flexible disc, a lever, a (3)_____ which takes in seawater, a set of (4)_____, many seawater pipes, a (5)_____ on the land
MAIN SPECIFICATIONS: 4.6 m (H) × (6)_____ m (L); pipe (7)_____ mm (W); pressure (8)_____ kPa (1000 psi); can generate (9)_____ kW of electricity
OPERATION: wave oscillates → pushes disc (10)_____ → lever oscillates → pistons push water through pipe at (11)_____ pressure → turbine (12)_____ → generates electricity
BENEFITS: Wave energy is a (13)_____ energy resource; uses no fossil fuels

TASK » 8 Work in small groups. Find out about one of these wave energy systems. Prepare a presentation about your system.

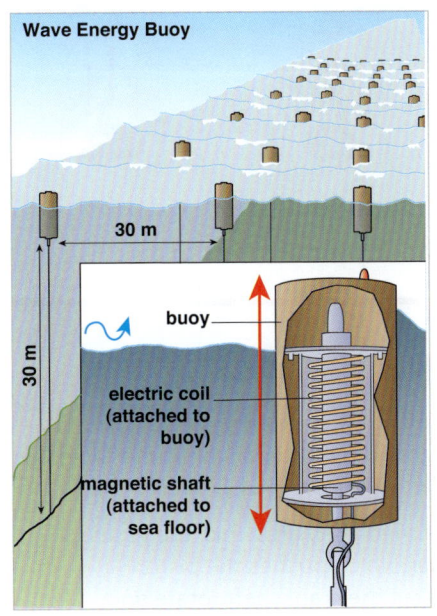
Wave Energy Buoy

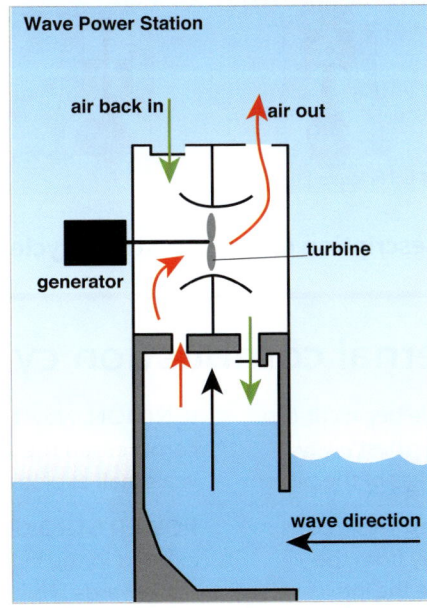
Wave Power Station

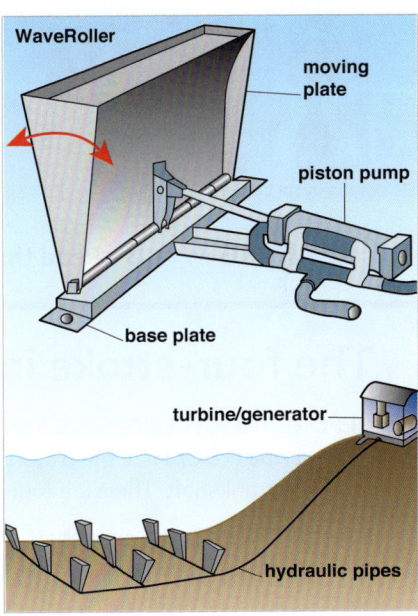
WaveRoller

Group 1. Turn to page 112 for your notes about the *Wave Energy Buoy*. (1)
Group 2. Turn to page 114 for your notes about the *Wave Power Station*. (2)
Group 3. Turn to page 116 for your notes about the *WaveRoller*. (3)

9 With your group, give a presentation about your system to the class. Answer questions from the class.

WRITING » 10 Write a description of your group's system, explaining how it works.

2 Engines

START HERE »

1 Work with a partner or in small groups. Draw arrows to show all the movements in this diagram of an internal-combustion engine cylinder.

2 Describe the motion of all the moving parts in the diagram. Use the words in the box.

> linear   oscillating   reciprocating   rotary

3 Explain what causes the movements of
- the valves
- the piston
- the crankshaft

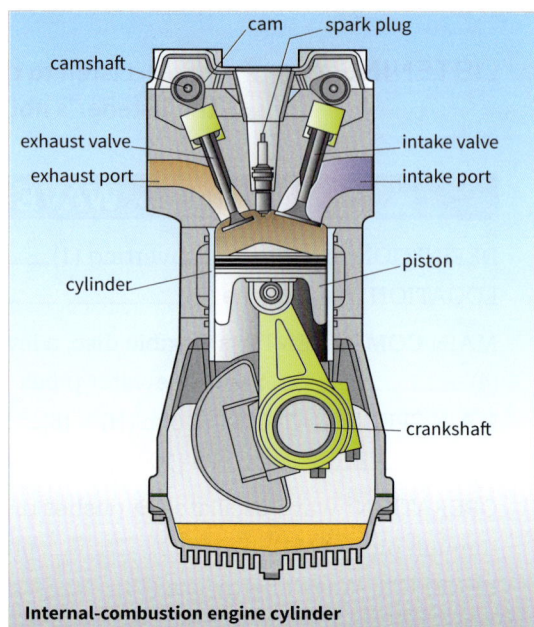

Internal-combustion engine cylinder

TASK »

4 With your partner or group, number these diagrams in the correct order.

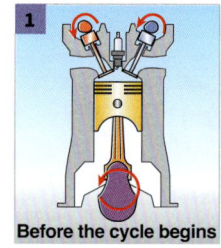
Before the cycle begins

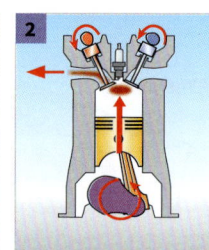

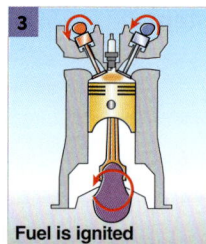
Fuel is ignited

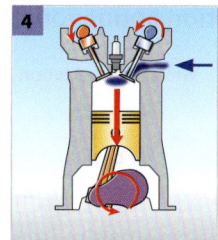

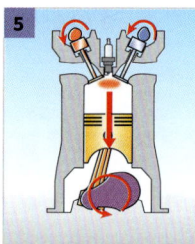

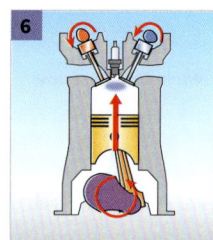

READING »

5 Read this description of the four-stroke cycle. Check your answers to 4.

The four-stroke internal combustion cycle

BEFORE THE CYCLE BEGINS. The cycle begins at *top dead centre* (TDC). Here the piston is furthest away from the crankshaft. There are four *strokes* of the piston.

INTAKE STROKE. The crankshaft rotates. This makes the piston move down the cylinder, away from the valves. At the same time, the cam above the intake valve rotates. This makes the valve move downwards, which opens the intake port. As the piston moves down, fuel is sucked into the cylinder through this inlet.

COMPRESSION STROKE. As the crankshaft rotates, it makes the piston move up the chamber towards the valves. Simultaneously, the cam above the intake valve rotates and allows it to close. Both valves are now closed. As the piston moves up towards the valves, it compresses the fuel.

IGNITION. Now the piston is once again at TDC. The compressed fuel is ignited by the spark plug and there is a small explosion at the top of the cylinder.

POWER STROKE. Immediately after this, the gases expand in the cylinder, which pushes the piston downwards. This makes the crankshaft rotate and provides torsion to drive the wheels of the vehicle.

EXHAUST STROKE. As the crankshaft rotates, it pushes the piston up the cylinder. At the same time, the cam above the exhaust valve pushes the valve downwards. This opens the exhaust port and the burnt gases are pushed out.

The cycle is repeated thousands of times per minute.

6 What do these words refer to?

1. *which* (line 9)   a) the cam b) the rotation of the cam
                         c) the movement of the valve
2. *it* (line 15)   a) the cam b) the intake valve c) the rotation of the cam
3. *this* (line 21)   a) the small explosion b) the top of the cylinder
4. *which* (line 22)   a) the cylinder b) the expansion of the gases
5. *This* (line 28)   a) the cam b) the port c) the movement of the valve

7 Find words in the text that mean the same as these phrases.

1. at the same time (one word)
2. twisting force (one word)
3. inlet which allows fuel to enter the cylinder (two words)
4. device which moves to allow gases to escape (two words)

LANGUAGE »

When often indicates that two actions happen in sequence, i.e. immediately after the other, e.g. *When the spark plug ignites, the gases explode*.

As often indicates that two actions happen simultaneously, i.e. both at the same time, e.g. *As the piston moves up, it compresses the fuel*.

When or *as* can sometimes be used with the same meaning when it's difficult to decide if two actions are simultaneous or in rapid sequence, e.g. *When/As the brake pedal is pressed, the piston pushes the oil along the brake pipe*.

8 Join each group of sentences into a single sentence. Use **when/as** and **which**. Do not use the words in italics.

1. The piston moves up. *At the same time*, the exhaust valve opens. This lets the burnt gases escape.
2. The spark plug ignites the fuel. *Immediately afterwards*, there is an explosion. This makes the piston move down with great force.
3. The camshaft rotates. *Simultaneously*, the cam pushes the intake valve downwards. This allows the fuel to enter the cylinder.
4. The piston moves away from the valves. *Immediately after this*, it creates a vacuum in the cylinder. This sucks the fuel in.
5. The piston moves up towards the valves. *Soon afterwards*, it puts the fuel under high pressure. This helps the gases to expand rapidly after ignition.
6. The cam pushes the exhaust valve down. *At the same time*, the piston moves up towards it. This forces the burnt gases out of the engine.

Example: *1 As the piston moves up, the exhaust valve opens, which lets the burnt gases escape.*

WRITING »

9 This is a diagram of an internal combustion engine that uses hydrogen as a fuel. Describe this engine and explain how it works. Explain the benefits of this kind of engine.

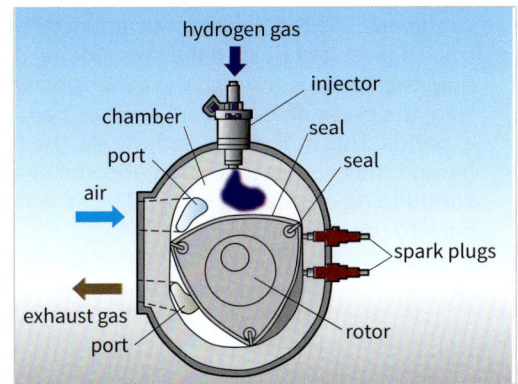

3 Cooling and heating

START HERE »

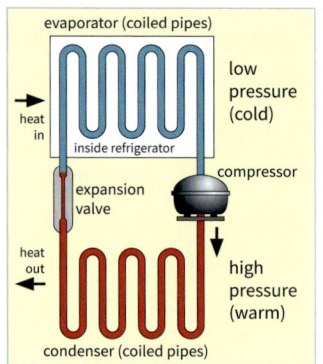

1 Discuss this question in groups. Which two scientific principles are refrigerators based on? Choose two from this list.

1. For every action there is an equal but opposite reaction.
2. When you compress a gas, it condenses. When you decompress a liquid, it evaporates.
3. The upthrust is equal to the weight of the displaced fluid.
4. As a gas condenses, it gives out heat. As a liquid evaporates, it absorbs (takes in) heat.

2 With your group, make notes about what happens to the fluid during a refrigeration cycle. Use the two principles from 1.

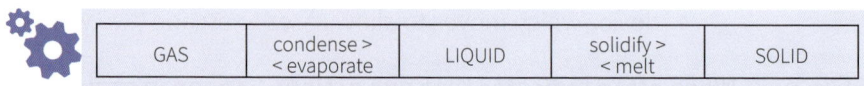

READING »

3 Read this description of a heat pump, and complete the diagram below.
- Draw an arrow on the pipes to show the direction of flow of the fluid.
- Delete the words *high* or *low* in the brackets.

HEAT PUMPS

A heat pump is an electrical device that pumps heat from one place to another. During cold weather, it extracts heat from the outside air and transfers it into the building. During hot weather, the heat pump reverses this operation and transfers heat from inside the building to the outside.

The machine is based on the two principles of the refrigeration cycle: (1) when a gas is compressed, it condenses and gives out heat, and (2) when a liquid is expanded, it evaporates and absorbs (or takes in) heat.

The main parts of a heat pump are a compressor, an expansion valve, two fans, a reversing valve and two sets of coils, one on the outside and the other on the inside of the building. The coils are thin pipes which are bent in a U shape many times. They can absorb and give out heat.

The compressor pumps a special fluid called a refrigerant around the coils. The refrigerant is under high pressure as it flows from the compressor to the condenser. As the fluid passes around the condenser coils, it gives out heat to the surrounding air. The fluid then passes through the expansion valve. Here the pressure is suddenly reduced and the fluid expands. This makes it evaporate. As the fluid passes around the evaporator coils, it absorbs heat from the surrounding air, making it cold. Then the fluid flows back to the compressor.

HEATING OPERATION

In cold weather, the outside coil acts as the evaporator and the inside coil acts as the condenser. The fluid in the evaporator is under low pressure and so it evaporates. The fan pulls the outside air over the evaporator and the fluid absorbs heat from it. The compressor then pumps the heated fluid into the building under high pressure to the condenser. The second fan blows air over the condenser and the heated air is blown into the building.

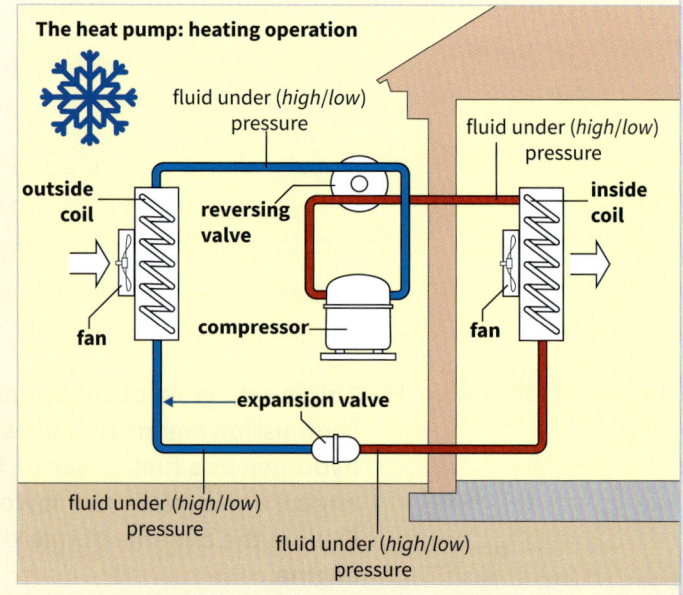

4   **Match the parts with their definitions.**

1 expansion valve   a) coiled pipes that give out heat to the surrounding air
2 coils   b) a pump which compresses the refrigerant
3 condenser   c) a device that decompresses the refrigerant
4 refrigerant   d) a fluid which evaporates at a low temperature
5 evaporator   e) pipes that carry the refrigerant around the system
6 compressor   f) coiled pipes that extract heat from the surrounding air

VOCABULARY »

5   **Make a table for all the words in the box. Use a dictionary if necessary.**

compress   condense   decompress   evaporate   extract   operate   refrigerate

Verb	Concept noun	Agent noun
compress	compression	compressor

WRITING »

6   **Continue and complete this description of the cooling operation of the heat pump.**

Cooling operation
During hot weather, the operation of the heat pump is reversed. The reversing valve changes the machine from a heater to an air conditioner. The outside coil then acts as …

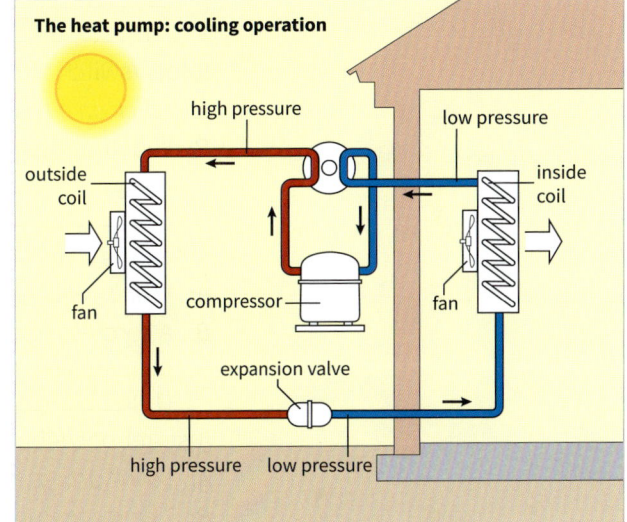

The heat pump: cooling operation

TASK »

7   **Work in small groups. Discuss this geothermal pump. Make notes about**

- its function
- how it works
- how it is different from the heat pump

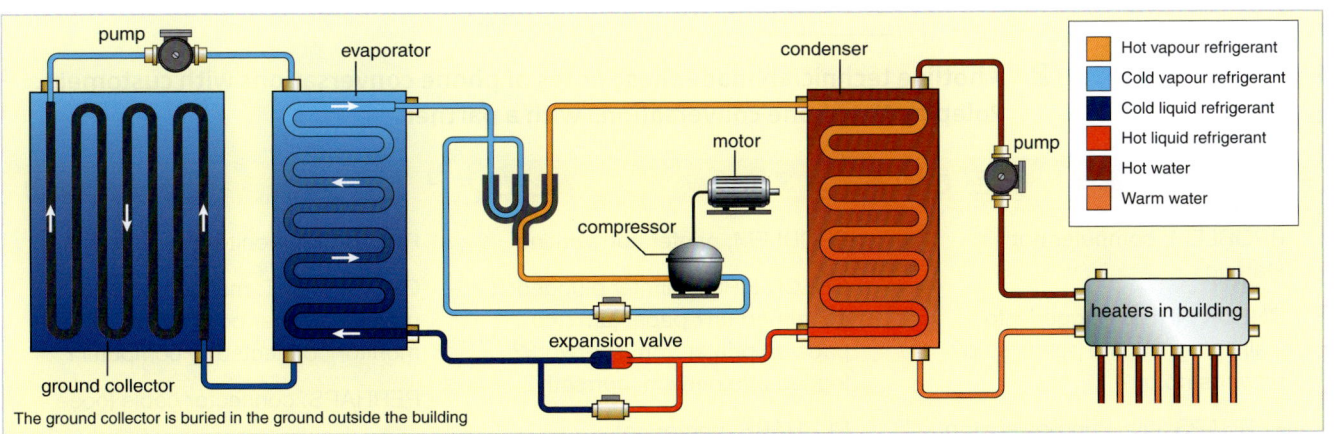

The ground collector is buried in the ground outside the building

8   **Write a description of the geothermal pump and how it works.**

Review Unit D

1 **Complete these phone conversations. Use the correct form of the verbs in brackets.**

1 (remember/check/uncheck/type)
   A: *I can't log into my company network. My password was rejected.*
   B: Your network system must be (1) <u>remembering</u> the wrong password. You might have (2) <u>checked</u> the **REMEMBER PASSWORD** box. Try (3) _____ this feature. Then try (4) _____ in the correct password again.

2 (block/lower/open)
   A: *I can't open my email attachments.*
   B: Your email program must be (5) _____ the attachments. Try (6) _____ your security settings. Then you can try (7) _____ the attachments again.

3 (block/switch off/empty)
   A: *I click on a link on a web page, but the link doesn't pop up.*
   B: Your firewall might have (8) _____ the pop-up. Try (9) _____ the **BLOCK POP-UPS** option in your firewall and then try (10) _____ your cache.

4 (interfere/take/move)
   A: *I can't get a wireless connection between my computer and my router.*
   B: A cordless phone or other device might be (11) _____ with the connection. Try (12) _____ the phone away. Or why don't you (13) _____ the router to another location?

5 (use/reboot/reboot/reboot)
   A: *I can't access the internet with my wireless router.*
   B: The router must be (14) _____ the wrong IP address. Why don't you (15) _____ the router first. If that doesn't work, try (16) _____ the computer and then you could (17) _____ the router again.

2 **A hotline technician made these notes of phone conversations with customers. Roleplay the phone conversations with a partner.**

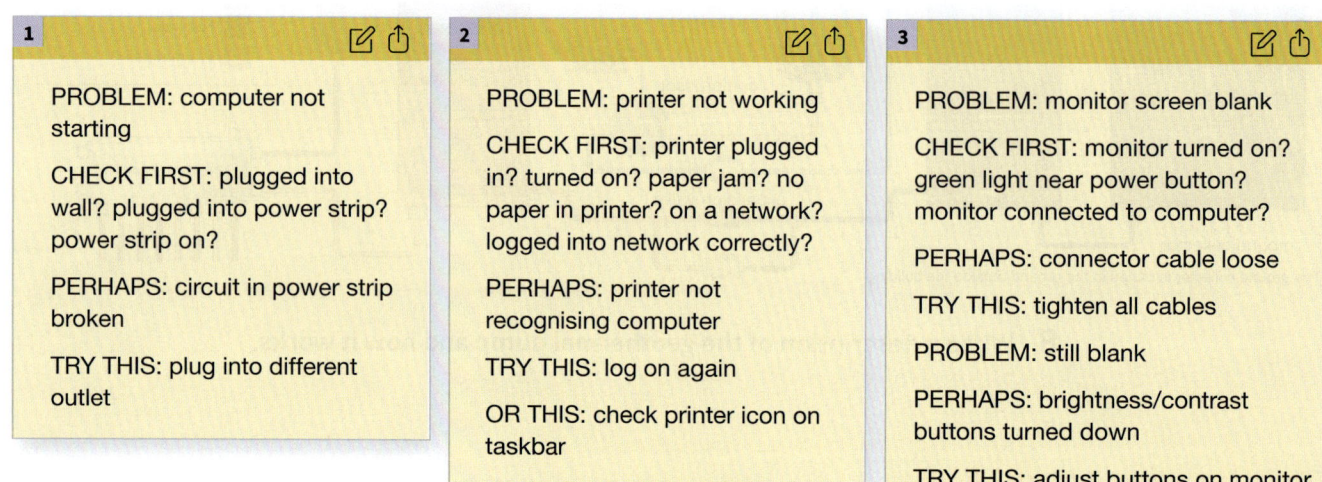

1

PROBLEM: computer not starting

CHECK FIRST: plugged into wall? plugged into power strip? power strip on?

PERHAPS: circuit in power strip broken

TRY THIS: plug into different outlet

2

PROBLEM: printer not working

CHECK FIRST: printer plugged in? turned on? paper jam? no paper in printer? on a network? logged into network correctly?

PERHAPS: printer not recognising computer

TRY THIS: log on again

OR THIS: check printer icon on taskbar

3

PROBLEM: monitor screen blank

CHECK FIRST: monitor turned on? green light near power button? monitor connected to computer?

PERHAPS: connector cable loose

TRY THIS: tighten all cables

PROBLEM: still blank

PERHAPS: brightness/contrast buttons turned down

TRY THIS: adjust buttons on monitor

3 What do you think *may / might / could / must* have caused the events in the photos to happen? Tell the class.

Example: *I think lightning must have struck this tree.*

4 Discuss how a two-stroke engine works with a partner.

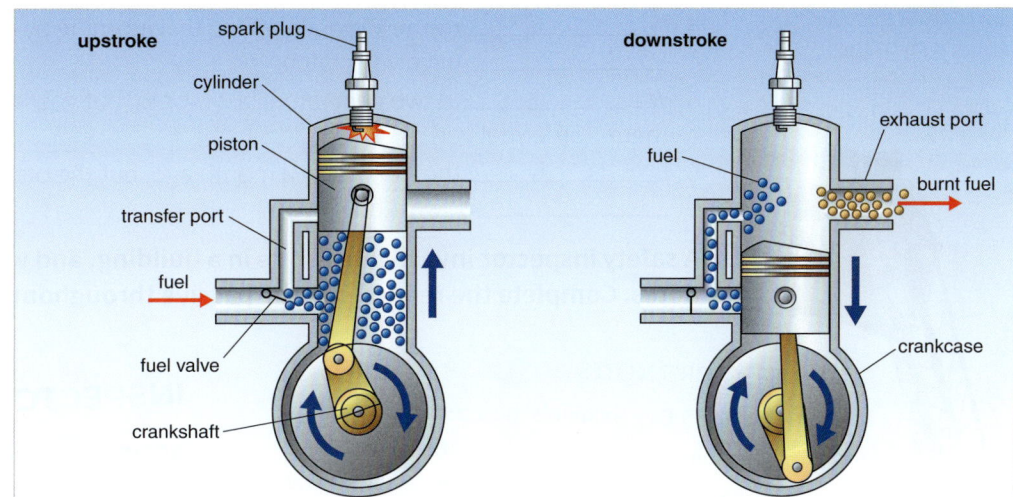

5 Put these sentences into the correct order.

Two-stroke engine: the upstroke

As a result, fresh fuel is sucked into the crankcase.
The vacuum opens the fuel valve.
When it reaches the top, the spark plug fires.
This compresses the fuel in the cylinder.
As the crankshaft rotates, it drives the piston up. **1**
Then the downstroke begins.
At the same time, it creates a vacuum in the crankcase.
Meanwhile, the piston moves up towards the top of the cylinder.

6 Use the information in these notes to write a paragraph describing the *downstroke* of the two-stroke engine.

Use *when* or *as* where possible to join two lines together. You can also use other words such as *meanwhile*.

Two-stroke engine: the downstroke	
1 spark plug fires	7 piston uncovers exhaust port
2 fuel ignites	8 piston reaches bottom of cylinder
3 this drives piston down	9 piston uncovers transfer port
4 piston moves down	10 fuel flows from crankcase
5 compresses fuel in crankcase	11 fuel flows into cylinder
6 piston moves down more	12 fresh fuel pushes out exhaust gas

Begin: When the spark plug fires, the fuel ignites. This drives the piston down. As it moves …

Review Unit D   65

7 Complete the sentences with the correct form of the verbs in brackets.

1 My new washing machine has _____. (break down)
2 My new car was _____ yesterday. The mirrors are _____. (deliver/crack)
3 You have _____ me the wrong shipment. (send)
4 I _____ my new mobile phone this morning by courier. The screen was _____. (receive/scratch)
5 We _____ two generators last month, but you have not _____ them. (order/deliver)
6 I _____ the motorbike a month ago, but the brakes have already _____ down. (buy/wear)

8 A safety inspector investigates a fire in a building, and writes a report from his notes. Complete the report. Use the passive throughout.

INSPECTOR'S NOTES

THINGS TO DO: examine the site of the fire ... inspect joints and connections ... test the main lift ... measure gaps between beams ... take away and test parts of the wall ... inspect all fire exits

DAMAGE: the fire destroys four storeys ... it shears three metal beams ... it twists the main column ... it jams two lifts ... it blocks two fire exits ... the heat cracks a large water tank (for sprinklers)

I RECOMMEND: reinforce structural columns ... strengthen water tanks ... provide backup power system ... install CCTV and monitors ... widen stairs ... cover ceilings with fireproof material

INSPECTOR'S REPORT

ACTIONS TAKEN
1 The site of the fire was examined.
2 Joints and connections were inspected.
3 ...

FINDINGS
1 Four storeys were destroyed by the fire.
2 Three metal beams were sheared.
3 ...

RECOMMENDATIONS
1 Structural columns should be reinforced.
2 Water tanks should be strengthened.
3 ...

9 You are the manager of Technik Ltd. Reply to this email.

To the Manager, Technik Ltd

Dear Sir or Madam

Hotspot washing machine: order no. TT/893166

I am writing to complain about the Hotspot washing machine that I ordered from your city centre shop two weeks ago. The washing machine was delivered ten days ago and it was installed by your service staff on the same day. It worked when the service person switched it on, but when I switched it on again the next day, there was a loud crash and then the machine stopped. I called the service hotline, but there was no reply for two days. Finally, I sent an email to customer services. The washing machine was taken away this morning, one week late. I am not satisfied with the washing machine or the service from your company. I look forward to hearing from you.

Misha Williams

10   Work in pairs or in small groups. Choose one of the two types of Stirling engine. Decide how it works.

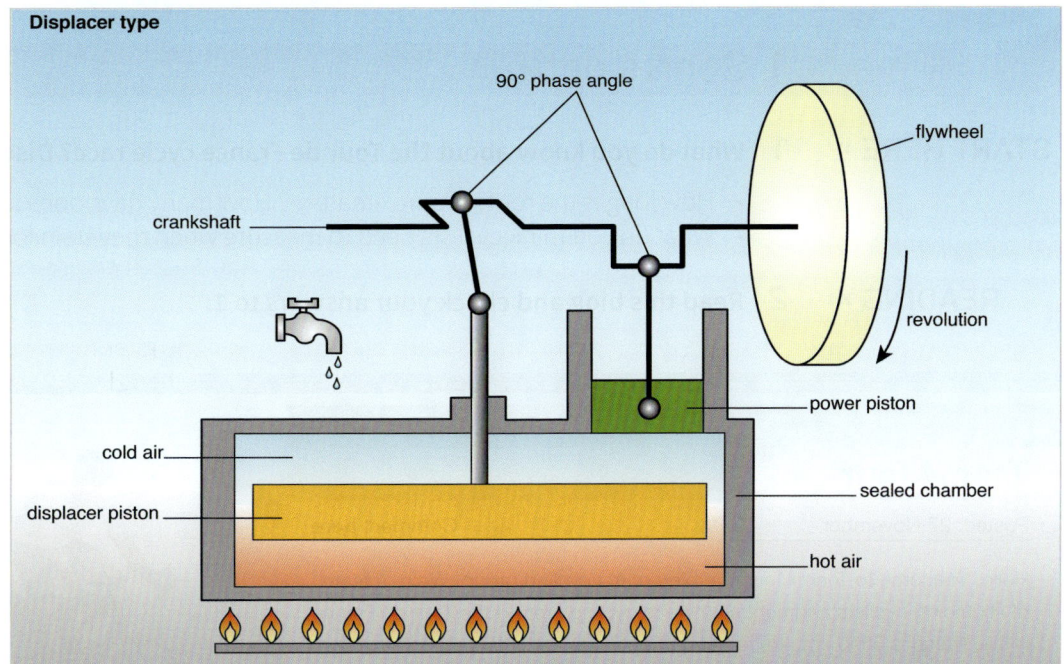

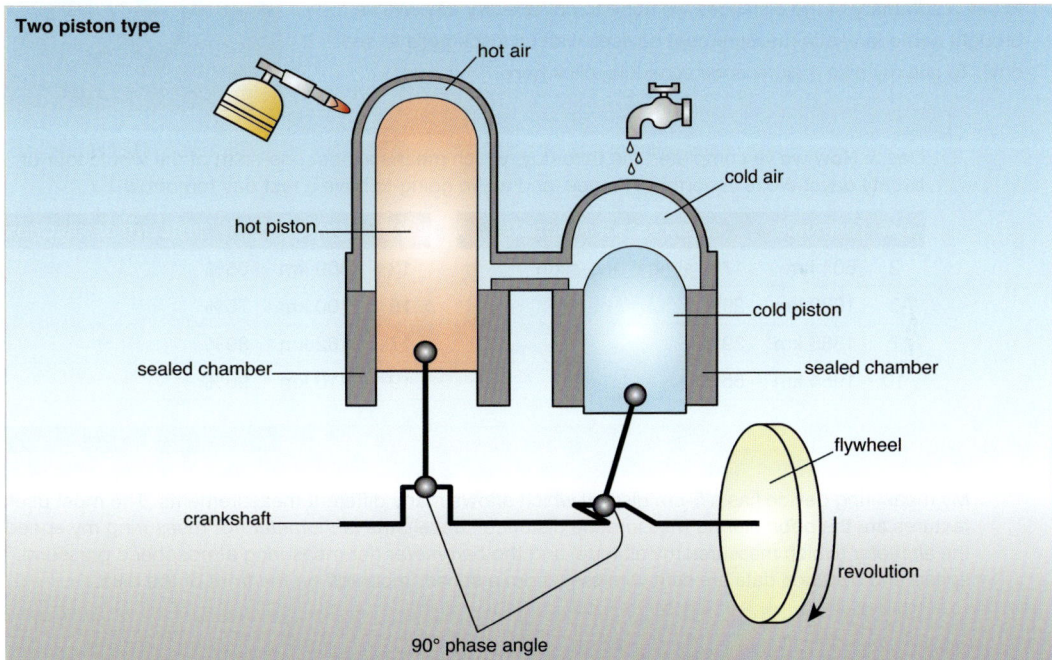

11   Write a description of the two engines and how they work.

PROJECT » 12   Find out about an important engine or piece of equipment used in your industry. Get information about
  - the principle behind it
  - the function of the main parts
  - how it works

13   Give a short talk about this to the class.

9 Measurement

1 Sports data

START HERE » 1 What do you know about the Tour de France cycle race? Discuss in pairs.
- How long is the route (approximately)? How many days does it take?
- What do you think cyclists need to measure when they train for a race?

READING » 2 Read this blog and check your answers to 1.

Team4Tour

Posted: 27 November   Comment **here**

Hello. Welcome to Team4Tour, the blog of my cycling group. We're a team of six racing cyclists and right now we're cycling around the Tour de France route, which is 3553 km. We're not competing in the actual race this year (maybe next year …). Right now, we're only practising the route. Click **here** to see a summary of the distances we hope to cover every day. We've brought some fantastic measurement devices with us (click **here** to see one). To see my bike maintenance schedule, click **here**.

Day 3. Now we've completed the third day, which means almost one-sixth of the whole tour of twenty days! We're in northern France, and we're going to have a rest day tomorrow …

DAY	DISTANCE	PERCENTAGE/FRACTION	DAY	DISTANCE	PERCENTAGE/FRACTION
3	604 km	17% almost one-sixth	13	2309 km	65%
5	1030 km	29%	15	2700 km	76%
7	1386 km	39%	17	3162 km	89%
10	1954 km	55%	19	3410 km	96%

My measuring device has a 5-cm display which shows many different measurements. The most useful features are the *odometer* (to measure the distance I travel), the *tachometer* (for measuring my speed), the *altimeter* (which measures my altitude) and the *barometer* (for measuring atmospheric pressure). The speed and distance data are sent wirelessly from a sensor mounted on the front of the bike.

After every ride.* * ride = day of cycling	Inflate tyres. Make sure that they are at the correct pressure. Examine tyres for wear. Worn tyres cause accidents. Check that the quick-release levers on the wheels are tight. I don't want wheels to fall off!
After every third ride (or every 500 km, whichever is sooner)	Test brakes and gears. Check that they are adjusted correctly. Inspect the saddle. Ensure that it is tight and at the correct height. I don't want it to slip down.
Every tenth ride (or when bike is wet)	Wash and dry bike. Apply oil carefully to chain and gears. Check that there's no lubricant on the wheel rims, to prevent brakes from slipping.

3 **Answer these questions on the text.**

1 What instruments provide data to measure: (1) How fast am I cycling? (2) How far have I cycled today? (3) How high am I above sea level?
2 When you inspect the (1) tyres (2) quick-release levers (3) saddle (4) wheel rims, what problems are you trying to prevent?
3 A cyclist has completed 520 km in two days of cycling. Should he/she test the gears now?

VOCABULARY »

4 **Match the sports measuring instruments with the other items in the table.**

Measuring instrument	What is measured	Unit of measurement	Abbreviation
1 barometer	distance (cycling)	metres	km/h
2 tachometer	speed	seconds	m
3 odometer	height (above sea level)	beats per second	km
4 altimeter	rate of heart beat	kilopascals	bps
5 stop watch	weight	watts	s
6 heart rate monitor	power output	kilograms	W
7 power monitor	pressure	kilometres per hour	kPa
8 scales	time	kilometres	kg

5 **Ask and answer questions about the table.**

What do you use for measuring your power output? What does kPa stand for? What's the abbreviation for beats per second? What's a tachometer used for? What does a barometer measure?

6 **What units of measurement and measuring instruments do you use in your technical field? Make a table. Use the headings from 4. Ask and answer questions about it, as in 5.**

7 **Complete the distance table in the blog in 2 with the words in the box. Use approximate fractions.**

| almost   approximately   just under   just over   more than   nearly |

8 **Make some statements using fractions about yourself, or about a topic which interests you.**

Example: *I've completed just under two-thirds of my training.*

READING »

9 **Read the text and answer the questions below.**

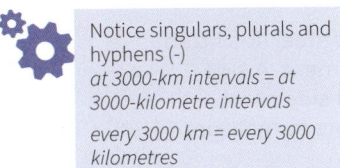

Notice singulars, plurals and hyphens (-)
at 3000-km intervals = at 3000-kilometre intervals
every 3000 km = every 3000 kilometres

Change the oil and filter, and lubricate moving parts every six months, or at 6000-mile intervals, whichever is the sooner. Service the battery after 54 months or 54,000 miles, whichever is the sooner. The brakes should be inspected and serviced (if necessary) at three-month intervals or every 3000 miles, whichever is the sooner.

1 A car has done 54,000 miles, but only 50 months. Should the battery be serviced now?
2 A car has done 30 months and 28,256 miles. The driver has inspected the brakes nine times. The last time was three months ago. Should the brakes be inspected again now?

9 Measurement

2 Sensors

START HERE »

1 Which of the following is *not* a sensor? Why not?

 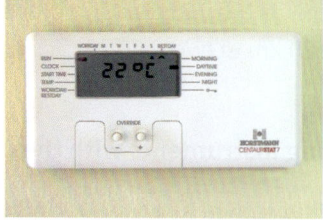  

2 What other sensors can you think of?

3 With a partner, write a definition of a sensor. Use these or other words.

sensor, device, detect, change (n), environment, convert, data

Begin: A sensor is …

READING »

4 Discuss with your partner.
- What's happening here?
- What are the engineers trying to measure?
- What kind of sensors are used?

5 Read this article and complete the statements below using these words: *acceleration*, *load*, *motion*.

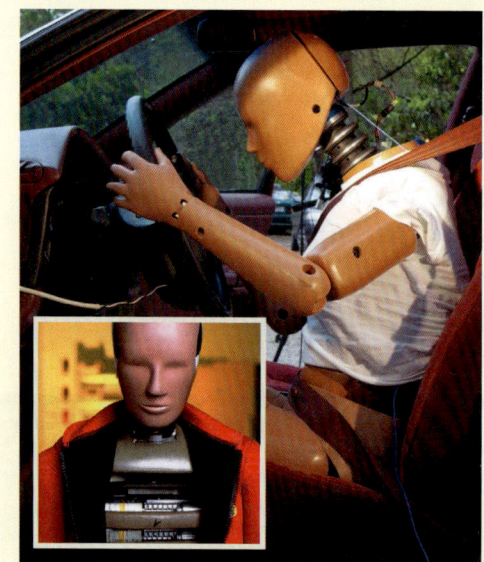

Two different crash test dummies are used in standard European vehicle crash tests. The first dummy is used for front impact crashes, and the second one is a side impact crash dummy. The dummies, which are made of steel, aluminium and rubber, contain many sensors.

Three types of sensing equipment are used: *acceleration sensors*, *load sensors* and *motion sensors*. The dummy heads contain three accelerometers (single direction acceleration sensors), which are set at right angles (forward-backward, up-down, and left-right). The dummy necks contain load sensors to detect the bending forces, shear forces and tension forces, which put pressure on the neck in a crash. The dummy legs contain load sensors, which measure the bending, shear, compression and tension forces on the leg.

In addition, a front impact crash test dummy has steel ribs fitted with motion sensors which record front rib movement. A side impact dummy has motion sensors which record side chest deflection (or inward movement), and load sensors to measure compression forces on the chest.

Three types of sensors are used in crash test dummies:

1 _____ sensors measure deflection (inward movement) of a body part during a crash.

2 _____ sensors measure how much a body part increases or decreases speed during a crash.

3 _____ sensors measure the force or pressure on a body part during a crash.

VOCABULARY » 6 Match the diagrams with (a) the names of the forces and (b) their descriptions.

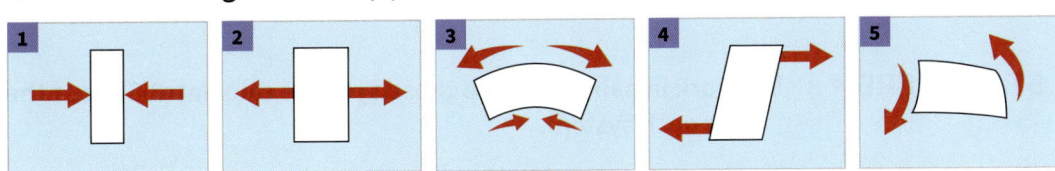

(a) bending, compression, shear, tension, torsion
(b) squeezing or pressing together; sliding in opposite directions; stretching or pulling apart; twisting; squeezing one side + stretching the other side

LANGUAGE » Noun + noun combinations are very common in technical English.

Examples: *acceleration sensors* (= sensors which measure acceleration); *vehicle crash tests* (= tests which crash a vehicle to measure its safety); *a side impact crash dummy* (= a dummy which measures the impact from the side in a crash).

gas flow meter

engine speed dial

tyre pressure gauge

bass volume indicator

7 Find phrases in the article in 5 which mean the same as these. All the words in the phrases must be nouns.

1 forces which pull something apart
2 sensors which detect movement or motion
3 deflection of the side of the chest
4 crashes which are caused by an impact from the front
5 a dummy which is used for testing the impact of a crash from the front

8 Expand these phrases. You can change words and add information.

1 a gas flow meter = <u>a meter which measures/for measuring the flow of gas (along a pipe)</u>
2 an engine speed dial = _____
3 a tyre pressure gauge = _____
4 a bass volume indicator = _____
   _____
5 an air pressure sensor = _____
   _____
6 a fuel intake port = _____

9 Make full sentence definitions from 8.

Example: *1 A gas flow meter is a meter which measures the flow of gas along a pipe.*

TASK » 10 List some sensors used in your industry. Complete a table like this one. If possible, work in small groups with others from the same industry.

Industry: civil engineering and construction		
Name of sensor	**Function/Use**	**Application**
strain gauge	to measure deformation of structures	high-rise buildings, bridges, roads

11 Explain to the class about the sensors you have listed in your table.

In the field of civil engineering and construction, strain gauges are used for measuring the deformation of structures. They're used in high-rise buildings, bridges and roads, for example.

9 Measurement

3 Positioning

START HERE »

1 Work in pairs. What do these systems calculate? Choose the most important one for each system.

distance, speed, location, height, depth

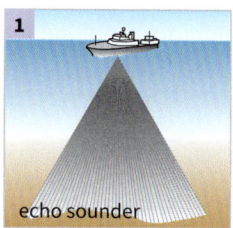
1 echo sounder

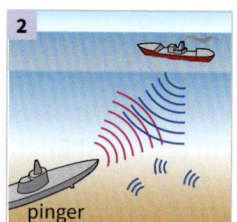
2 pinger

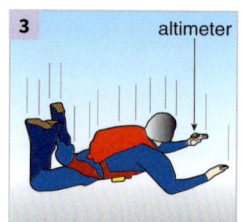
3 altimeter

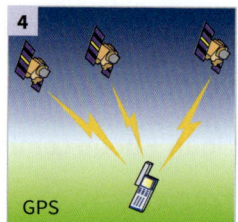
4 GPS

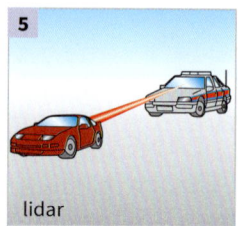
5 lidar

READING »

2 The footnotes on this web page are in the wrong order. Write the footnote numbers in the spaces.

What is GPS?

GPS stands for global positioning system. It can tell you **your precise location**[(1)] anywhere on (or above) the Earth to within six metres.

A group of 24 or more satellites orbit the Earth at an altitude of 11,000 miles. Every 12 hours, a satellite makes an orbit, or one complete cycle in space around the Earth. The satellites transmit signals to receivers on the ground.

The user has a GPS receiver, which detects the signals from the satellites, and calculates **their distance**[(2)] from the receiver. Receivers can be held in your hand or mounted in a vehicle, such as a car or ship. A hand-held receiver is about the size of a mobile phone, but the newer models are even smaller. For instance, you can now buy one which is just 100 mm long.

How does the system work?

The satellites know **their precise position**[(3)] in their own orbits. Each satellite sends a signal to the receiver at the speed of light. This signal tells the receiver its exact location. In addition, it tells the receiver **the transmission time**[(4)] of the signal.

How does the receiver calculate how far it is from the satellite?

It subtracts the time when the signal was received (T_1) from the time when it was sent (T_2). Then it multiplies this number by the speed of light (c). This gives the distance (D) from the receiver to the satellite. However, to find out your exact location (that is, your longitude, latitude and altitude), your receiver needs signals from at least three satellites.

Why do you need at least three satellites to tell you where you are?

Each satellite transmits a different position and time signal to the receiver. The receiver is able to calculate its exact location (to within six metres) by comparing the three different signals.

Footnotes
(____) in other words, when it was sent
(____) that is, how far away they are
(____) or, exactly where you are
(____) i.e., exactly where they (the satellites) are

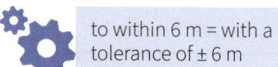
to within 6 m = with a tolerance of ± 6 m

3 Choose the correct calculation according to the text.

a) $D = (T_2 - T_1)/c$
b) $T_1 - (T_2 * c) = D$
c) $D = (T_2 - T_1) * c$
d) $T_2 - (T_1 * c) = D$

4 Choose the closest meaning for each word/phrase in the text. Choose from these meanings: **and, but, for example, in other words**.

1 *or* (line 7)
2 *such as* (line 13)
3 *For instance* (line 15)
4 *In addition* (line 21)
5 *However* (line 28)
6 *that is* (line 29)

LANGUAGE »

Please tell me I need to know This instrument can show you The computer calculates	**Noun phrase** your location. the depth of the river. the altitude of the planes.
	Indirect question where you are. how deep the river is. how high the planes are.

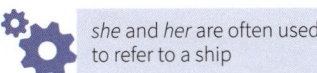
she and *her* are often used to refer to a ship

5 Replace the phrases in italics. Use the nouns in the box and add any necessary words.

> altitude   depth   distance   height   length   location   speed   temperature   width

1 Please find out *where the ship is*, and *how fast she is going*.
2 Before you touch the liquid, you should check *how hot it is*.
3 I want to find out *how far away the plane is* and *how high it is above sea level*.
4 Could you please tell me *how deep the river is* below the bridge.
5 I also need to know *how wide*, *how long* and *how high the bridge is*.

Example: *1 Please find out the location of the ship and her speed.*

6 Replace the phrases in italics. Use the word(s) in brackets.

1 All aeroplanes carry altimeters. These devices measure air pressure. From this reading, the altimeter can calculate *the height of the plane above sea level*. (how/high)
2 A submarine's pinger sends out a ping, or burst of sound, which is reflected back from ships in the sea. This allows the crew to find out *the location of the ships*. (where)
3 A lidar system can work out *the distance of a vehicle* from the device. It takes many readings as the vehicle approaches. From this it can calculate *the speed of the vehicle*. (how/far/fast)
4 An airport radar system sends out a sound signal which is reflected from an approaching plane. Since the system knows *the speed of the sound signal*, it can calculate *the distance of the plane* from the airport tower. (how/fast/far)

Example: *1 … the altimeter can calculate how high the plane is above sea level.*

TASK »

7 Work in groups.

- Brainstorm everyday applications which use GPS. Choose one that interests you.
- Prepare a short presentation, showing how GPS works in the application.
- Present your group's ideas to the rest of the class.

Some examples of the use of GPS include: *police, fire and emergency medical services*; *forest fire prevention*; *surveying and construction*; *tunnel digging*; *bridge building*; *mining*; *company cars*; *delivery vans*; *dealing with environmental disasters such as oil spills in the sea*; *air-sea rescue services*; *agriculture*; *animal herding*; *tracking endangered species*; *hiking and camping*; *sailing*.

10 Forces

1 Properties

START HERE »

1 This is a bridge in a severe storm, minutes before it collapsed. Identify the forces acting on it. Use the words in the box. If you need to, look again at the diagrams and questions in 6 on page 71.

| compression   shear   tension   torsion |

SCANNING »

2 Practise your speed reading. Look for the information you need on the SPEED SEARCH pages (118–119). Try to be the first to complete the task.

Task: Find information about the bridge in the photo in 1.
- What was the name of the bridge?
- In which year did it collapse?
- How strong was the wind?

READING »

3 Read these descriptions of tests and write the figure number in the gaps.

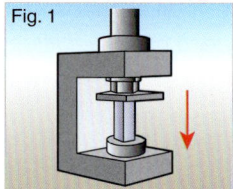
Fig. 1

Fig. 2

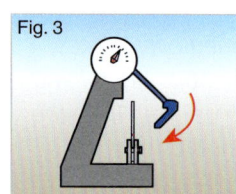
Fig. 3

Materials-testing: destructive tests

The purpose of the tensile strength test (**Fig.** _____) is to discover whether a material will *deform* (change shape) or break when it is pulled apart. The material is secured with two clamps, one at each end. The clamps are pulled apart with a specified force. The *yield point* (the point where the material deforms) and/or the *breaking point* (the point where the material breaks) is measured. This measurement shows you the tensile strength of the material.

The aim of the impact-resistance test (**Fig.** _____) is to find out whether a material will bend or break when it is struck with force. The bottom of the material is placed in a clamp, so that it stands vertically. A hammer strikes the material with a specified force. The yield point and/or the breaking point is measured. This indicates the impact resistance of the material.

The objective of the compressive strength test (**Fig.** _____) is to find out if a material will deform or break when it is compressed. The material is secured in a clamp between a fixed head and a moving head. The moving head presses down on the material and the load is increased. The yield point and/or the breaking point are measured. This indicates the compressive strength of the material.

4 Divide each paragraph in 3 into three sections. Use these headings.
- Objective
- Procedure
- Result

Example: **Objective**. *The purpose of the tensile strength test* … **Procedure**. *The material is secured* … **Result**. *This measurement shows you* …

LANGUAGE »

Aim	of	Process	is	to	Verb	if	Phrase
The aim The purpose The objective	of	the test the investigation	is	to	find out discover	if whether	the metal bends. the plastic breaks.

5 Change these questions into statements about objectives. Use each word/phrase at least once.

> aim   discover   find out   investigation   objective   purpose   test

1 Does this metal deform easily when it is hammered?
2 Is this material elastic or plastic when it is stretched?
3 Does this metal break when you strike it with a force of 10,000 newtons?
4 Will this plastic withstand deformation when it is heated to 120°C?
5 Do these three types of ceramic melt when they are heated to over 500°C?
6 Will this concrete beam crack when it is compressed under a weight of 5 tonnes?

Example: *1 The purpose of the test is to discover if this metal deforms easily when it is hammered.*

withstand = resist

VOCABULARY »

6 Underline the stressed syllable.

1 tens ile   tens ion
2 com press ive   com press ion
3 ri gid   ri gid i ty
4 flex i bil i ty   flex i ble
5 e las ti ci ty   e las tic
6 plas tic   plas ti ci ty

7 🔊 10.1 Listen and check your answers.

8 Make a table like this. Use all the words from 6.

Noun	Adjective	Noun	Adjective
tension	tensile	flexibility	flexible

TASK »

9 Work in groups. Choose one of the following tests on parts of a bicycle: (1) the wheel, (2) the saddle, (3) the frame. Discuss how to do the test. Make notes.

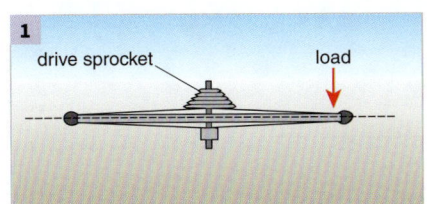
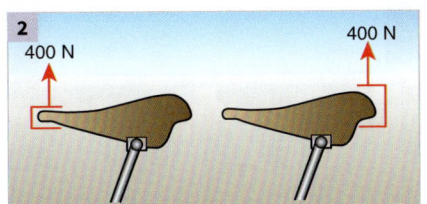
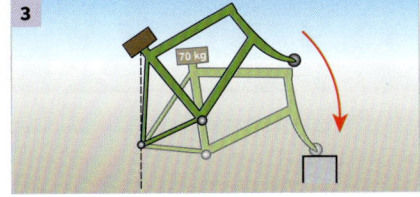

10 Work individually. Use the notes from your group work. Write your description of the test under three headings.

- Objective of test
- Procedure
- Result

11 Explain your group's test to the rest of the class.

10 Forces

2 Resistance

START HERE » 1 Work in small groups. Discuss these questions.
- How do earthquakes affect high-rise buildings?
- How do you think engineers make buildings resistant to earthquakes?

LISTENING » 2 🔊 10.2 Listen to part of a talk. What is the speaker mainly talking about in this part? Choose one:
- damage caused by earthquakes
- solutions to problems of earthquakes
- causes of earthquakes

3 Listen again and tick all the signpost phrases you hear.

Note: *signpost phrases* give directions to the listeners. They tell the listeners where they are in the talk.

Giving the purpose of the talk	Starting a new topic	Referring to visual
the main aim of this presentation is to	that brings me to	as you can see in the photo
the aim of my talk today is to	I'd like to begin by	as the slide shows
my objective in this talk is to	let's move on to	as shown in Figure 1

4 🔊 10.3 Listen to the next part of the talk. How many methods does the speaker mention? What *signpost phrases* does he use to introduce each method?

5 Label the three slides that the speaker refers to. Label them 1, 2 and 3.

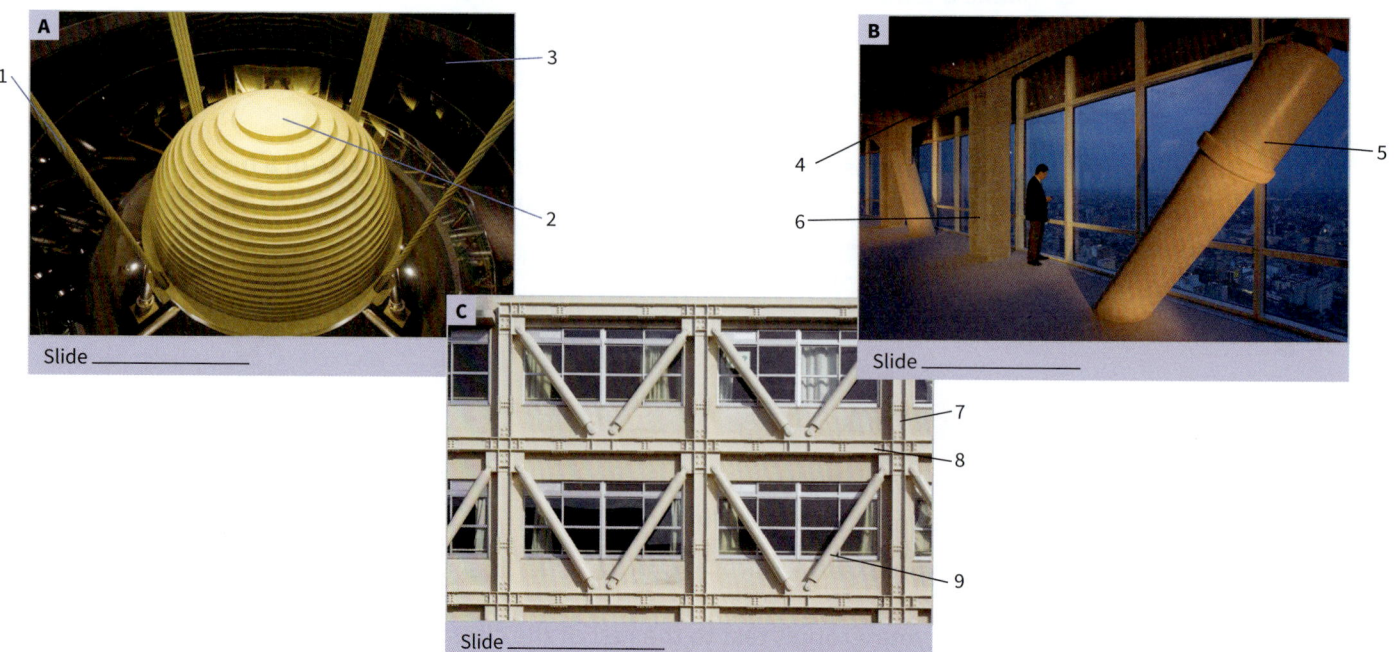

A Slide _____

B Slide _____

C Slide _____

READING » 6 Read the text and add labels to the parts in the photos in 5. Use the words in the box.

> beam(x2) brace steel cable TMD viscous damper column(x2) Taipei 101

Making buildings earthquake-resistant

1 Diagonal brace
The most common method is to strengthen the frame of the building using braces. A brace is a diagonal at the corner of a horizontal beam and a vertical column. The brace, beam and column form a truss, or triangular structure, which is very strong. However, it is also very rigid – it cannot be bent. This rigidity can also be a weakness, because rigid structures can be broken during the most powerful earthquakes.

2 Brace with damper
In this method, dampers are added to braces. A damper is a device that slows down movement. It consists of a piston that moves inside a cylinder filled with a viscous fluid such as silicone oil, which allows the piston to move, but slowly. When the earthquake strikes the foundations of a building, the frame of the building is able to move and bend slightly, but the movement is reduced by the action of the damper on the brace. The frame moves in a controlled way: it can be bent slightly, but is unbreakable.

3 Tuned massive damper (TMD)
In this method, the damper is a large mass, usually a sphere made of lead, such as the one at the top of the Taipei 101 building. This is suspended inside the building, near the top of the structure, where it acts as a pendulum. The mass is supported by steel cables. These cables are able to resist tension – they cannot be stretched. Dampers are placed between the mass and the building, so that the mass is able to move independently of the building. When an earthquake strikes, and the building starts to bend sideways, the pendulum moves in the opposite direction and neutralises the energy of the earthquake.

LANGUAGE » Here are some ways of expressing ability and inability when talking about properties:

Active: *The steel cables can resist tension. They are able to resist tension.*

Passive: *The cables cannot be stretched. They are unstretchable.*

Some adjectives have the suffixes *-able* and *-ible* with a passive meaning, e.g. *breakable* = able to be *broken* (= you can break it); *combustible* = able to be burnt (= you can burn it).

Negative prefixes, e.g. *non-/un-/in-*: *non-portable*, *unbreakable*, *inaudible* (= it cannot be heard).

-proof: *waterproof* (= able to keep water out completely).

-resistant: *heat-resistant* (= able to withstand heat)

7 Underline examples of the above in the text in 6.

   Example: *However, it is also very rigid – it <u>cannot be bent</u>*

8 Rewrite these sentences to give the same meaning. Use *can/cannot* and the correct form of the words in brackets.

   1 This plastic is heat-resistant and inflexible. (resist; bend)
   2 A cross brace is resistant to tension in two directions. (withstand)
   3 These sunglasses are scratchproof, but not impact-resistant. (scratch; break)
   4 The emergency generator is moveable by forklift but is not portable by hand. (move; carry)

   Example: *1 This plastic can resist heat and cannot be bent.*

3 Results

START HERE » 1 Test your knowledge of safe electrical circuits. Put a tick next to the people if they get electric shocks in these situations.

(The correct answers are on page 112)

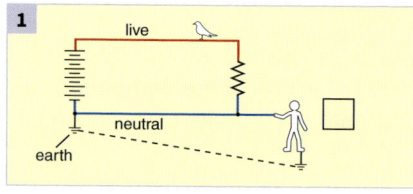
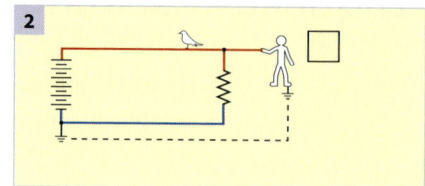
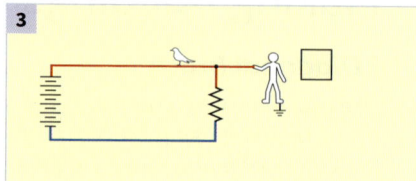
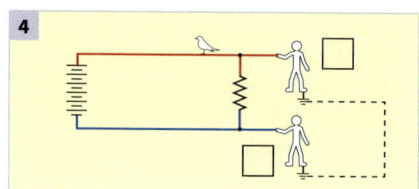
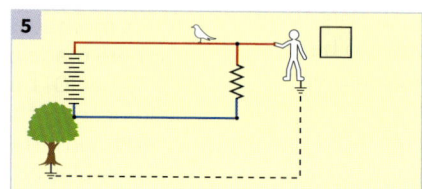
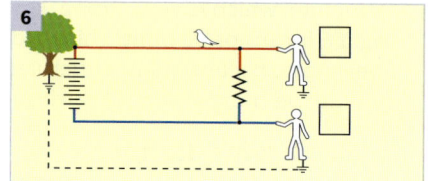

2 Work in groups. Discuss the reasons why people get (or don't get) electric shocks in the situations in 1. Explain your group's reasons to the class.

READING » 3 Read these captions. Write in the figure numbers of the diagrams they describe.

A Fig _____. The person gets a shock because they touch the live wire in an earthed system.

B Fig _____. This system is not earthed, but a tree touches the neutral wire and acts as an earth. The person touches the live wire. As a result, they get a shock.

C Fig _____. There are no trees in contact, and so this system is completely unearthed. Because two people touch a wire, they both get a shock.

D Fig _____. The person touches the neutral wire in an earthed system, and as a result they don't get a shock.

E Fig _____. As this system is not earthed, the person can touch any wire without a shock.

F Fig _____. In this non-earthed system, a tree touches the live wire and acts as an earth. Two people touch a wire. One touches the neutral wire and therefore gets a shock. The other touches the live wire; they are safe.

LANGUAGE » Expressing **cause**: *because, since, as*
Expressing **result** (or **effect**): *(and) so, (and) therefore, (and) as a result*

4 Replace the word(s) in italics with the word(s) in brackets. Make any necessary changes in punctuation and word order.

Example: *1 Ben touched an earthed live wire, and as a result he got a shock.*

1 Ben got a shock *because* he touched an earthed live wire. (*and as a result*)

2 Ron touched an earthed neutral wire, *and as a result* he was safe. (*because*)

3 *As* Bill touched an unearthed wire, he didn't get a shock. (*and so*)

4 Bob touched a live wire when a tree touched a neutral wire. *Therefore* he got a shock. (*because*)

5 Pete touched a live wire when a tree touched it. *So* he was safe. (*since*)

6 *Since* Tom and Del touched an unearthed wire, they got a shock. (*and therefore*)

VOCABULARY » A group of verbs contain the idea of cause as part of their meaning. They have the suffix *-en*, for example *strengthen* (= to cause something to be stronger).

Here is a list: *harden* (≠ *soften*), *lengthen* (≠ *shorten*), *lighten* (≠ *darken*), *strengthen* (≠ *weaken*), *tighten* (≠ *loosen*), *widen*, *flatten*, *sharpen*, *straighten*.

5 Replace the phrases in *italics* with phrases using verbs from the above list.
  1 The torsion forces in the storm must have *made the bridge weaker*.
  2 The purpose of adding carbon to steel is to *make it stronger*.
  3 Long ago, humans used stones to *make their knife blades sharper and straighter*.
  4 In forging, metal is heated to *make it softer*. Then it is put in water to *make it hard* again.
  5 Hot weather *makes railway lines longer* and cold weather *makes them shorter*.
  6 If the race has *made the bike saddle looser*, you should *make it tight* with a spanner.

Example: *1 The torsion forces in the storm must have weakened the bridge.*

TASK » 6 Work in small groups. Discuss this diagram with the rest of your group.

This is someone's theory of what might have caused the *Titanic* to sink so quickly. Do you agree with it? What else could have caused it?

7 Explain your group's opinion of the rivet theory to the rest of the class.

8 Work individually. Write an explanation of how faulty rivets could have caused the *Titanic* to sink so quickly. Use the notes and information from the diagram.

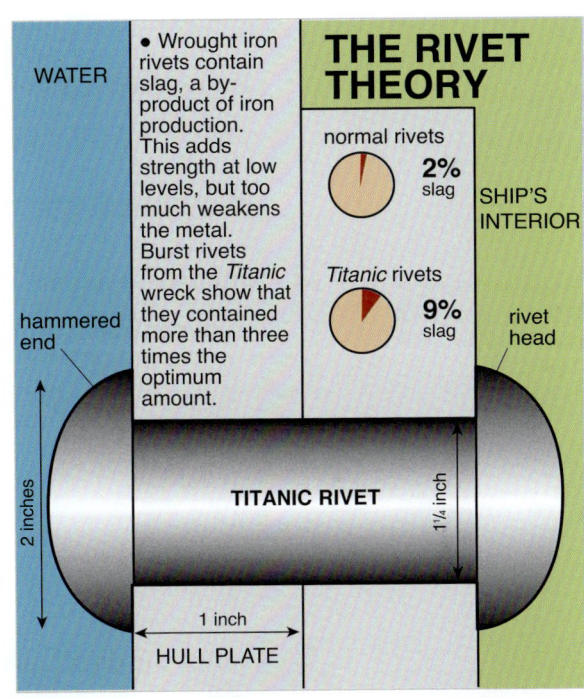

Dimensions of (a) hull plates (b) rivets
Percentage of slag in iron:
  (a) normal rivets (b) *Titanic* rivets

Effect of slag on iron (strengthen? weaken?):
  at low levels? at high levels?

Cause of damage
  1 iceberg hits hull → bending force on plate → shear force on rivets
  2 rivet head breaks → weakens other rivets
  3 extra load → good rivets break → water enters ship
  4 water fills 5 or 6 compartments → ship sinks too quickly

Result: *Carpathia* too late, can't rescue passengers

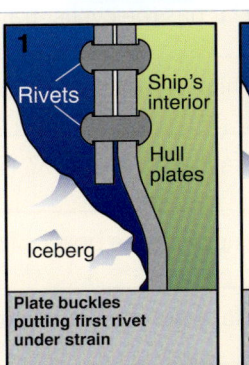 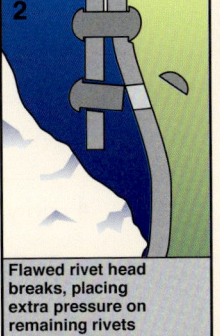 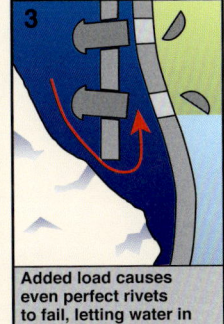

• Compartments at point of impact would have failed anyway, but five or six took on water. The ship could survive only four flooded compartments.
Better rivets would have saved some compartments, allowing *Titanic* to stay afloat for longer.

A slight delay in the sinking of *Titanic* would have allowed the rescue of all the passengers by *Carpathia*.

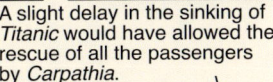

10 Forces

Review Unit E

1 This pie chart shows the percentage of students studying different subjects in a technical college. Describe the chart using fractions and approximations: *almost, less than, more than, just under, just over, nearly, approximately, exactly*

Begin: 1 Less than one-twentieth of the students are studying software engineering.

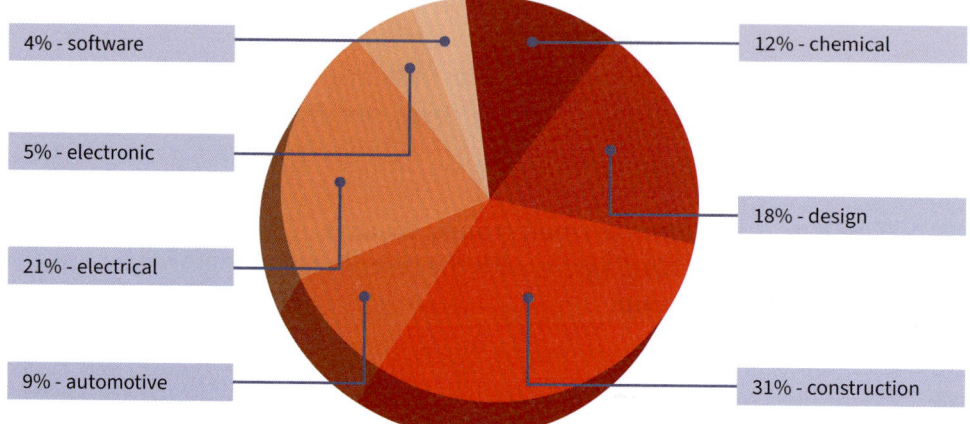

- 4% - software
- 5% - electronic
- 21% - electrical
- 9% - automotive
- 12% - chemical
- 18% - design
- 31% - construction

2 Match these items.

Instrument/Sensor	What is measured/detected
1 police lidar	a) weight
2 sound level meter	b) distance (away)
3 scales	c) distance (travelled)
4 radar	d) position
5 GPS	e) height
6 odometer	f) loudness
7 altimeter	g) speed

3 Change the direct questions into indirect questions.

1 How far has the cyclist travelled? (The odometer measures …)

2 How high is the plane above sea level? (The altimeter tells the pilot …)

3 How fast did the car go? (The lidar equipment told the police …)

4 How heavy is the boxer? (You should use these scales to check …)

5 How far were the planes from the tower? (The radar system indicated …)

6 Where are the motorboats? (The GPS system will tell you exactly …)

7 How loud were the guitars last night? (I used a sound level meter to find out …)

Example: *1 The odometer measures how far the cyclist has travelled.*

4 Change these questions into instructions. Use the verbs in brackets + *that*.

1 Are the brakes adjusted correctly? (make sure)
_____

2 Is the saddle tight and at the correct height? (check)
_____

3 Is there any lubricant on the wheel rims? (make sure/no lubricant)
_____

4 Are the wheel spokes all at the same tension? (ensure)
_____

Example: *1 Please make sure that the brakes are adjusted correctly.*

5 Fill in the gaps.

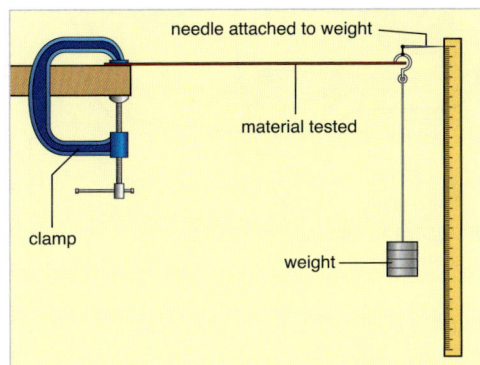

The aim of the rigidity test is (1) _____ (discover/to discover) if a material (2) _____ (deform/deforms) or (3) _____ (breaking/breaks) when it (4) _____ (is bending/is bent) by a force. One end of the material (5) _____ (secures/is secured) in a clamp, so that the material (6) _____ (holds/is held) horizontally with one end free. A weight (7) _____ (attaches/is attached) to the free end, and then the load (8) _____ (is increased/is increasing) by adding more weights. The breaking point (9) _____ (measures/is measured). This (10) _____ (shown/shows) us the rigidity of the material.

6 Match the sentences.

1 It's flexible.
2 It's rigid.
3 It's hard.
4 It's tough.
5 It's elastic.
6 It's heat-resistant.
7 It's strong in tension.
8 It's strong in compression.
9 It has torsional strength.

a) When you heat it, it doesn't burn or deform.
b) When you drop it or strike it, it doesn't break.
c) When you compress it, it doesn't break or deform.
d) When you twist it, it doesn't break or deform.
e) You can't bend it.
f) You can bend it, and it doesn't break.
g) You can stretch it and make it longer, but it doesn't break.
h) When you pull it, it doesn't stretch or break.
i) You can't scratch it or cut it.

7 Replace the phrases in italics with phrases using *make/made* + comparative adjective.

1 We need to bring some diggers here *to deepen the trench*.
_____

2 Last year's small earthquakes have *weakened the foundations*.
_____

3 The only way to *strengthen the walls* is to add braces between them.
_____

4 You have to *soften the metal* before you can hammer it into shape.
_____

Example: *1 We need to bring some diggers here to make the trench deeper.*

Review Unit E

8 Work in groups. Discuss these questions about the three car tests below.

- What is the purpose of each test?
- Which parts of the car are tested?
- What properties are tested?
- What is the procedure for each test? How is each test done?
- What measurements are made after the test?
- How does a car pass the test? What is a good result for the car?
- If a car fails a test, what would you recommend?

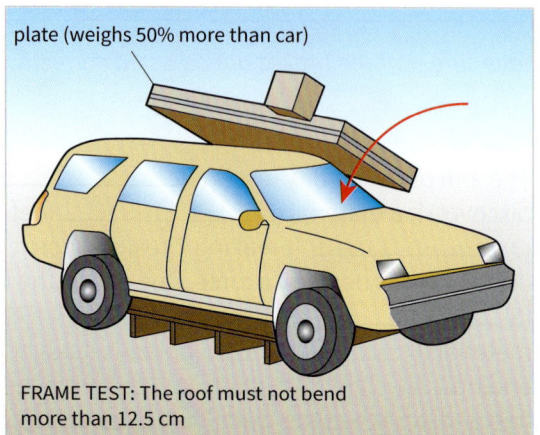

FRAME TEST: The roof must not bend more than 12.5 cm

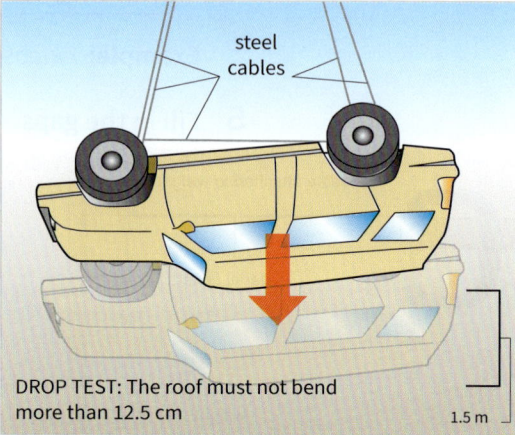

DROP TEST: The roof must not bend more than 12.5 cm

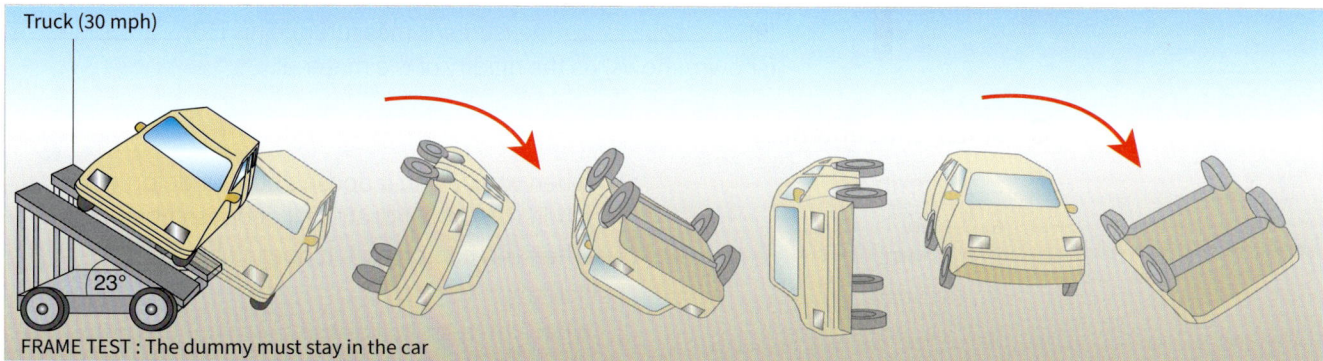

FRAME TEST : The dummy must stay in the car

9 Work individually. Use the notes from your group work. Write a description of the three tests, including this information

- the objectives of each test
- how to carry out each test
- how to pass each test

10 Here are the results of a new car model (the Sunburst XJ22) in the three tests. Write a short report.

- Explain the results of each test.
- Make recommendations.

NEW MODEL TESTED	Sunburst XJ22
TEST RESULTS	
FRAME TEST	roof bent 3.2 cm
DROP TEST	roof bent 12.8 cm
ROLL TEST	dummy was thrown 2.2 m from car

11 Work in small groups. Choose one of the natural disasters below. Discuss what you know about it. Search for information about what causes it, what the effects are and what technology can help. Make notes. You will need your notes for 12.

WILDFIRES

Technology that can help:
- wireless multi-sensor network in forests
- sensors + cameras measuring temperature, humidity, etc.
- big data: weather, computer modelling, satellite images
- drones surveying + extinguishing fire

FLOODING

Technology that can help:
- flood forecasting + alerts, e.g. Google in India, Bangladesh
- alerts and maps texted to smartphones
- sensors that trigger river barriers to rise
- LiDAR flood risk mapping and drones, e.g. in Thailand

TSUNAMIS

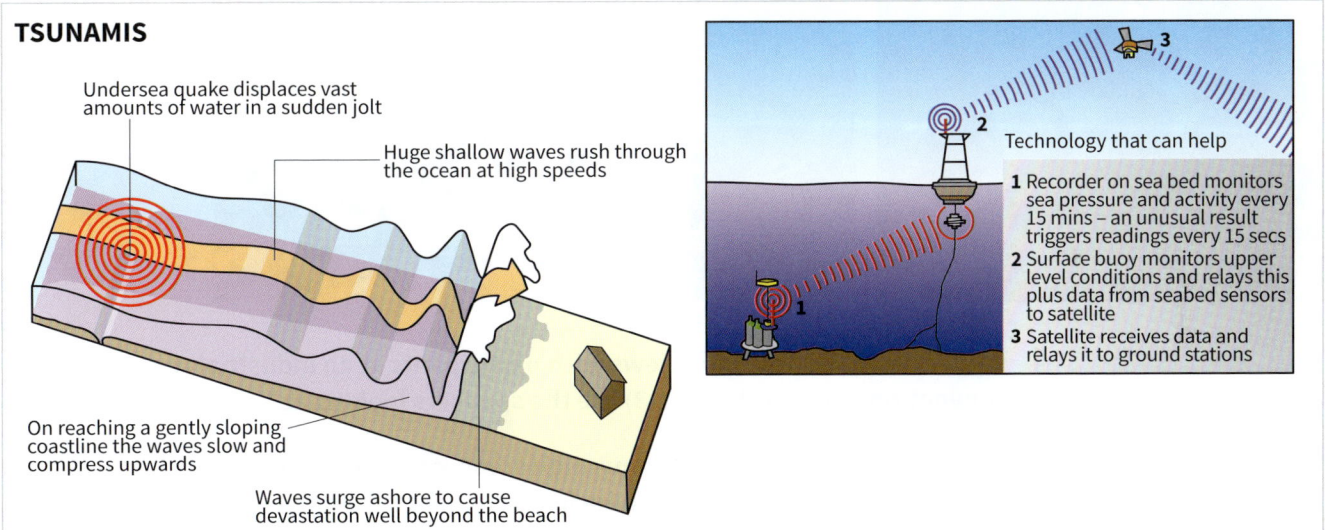

- Undersea quake displaces vast amounts of water in a sudden jolt
- Huge shallow waves rush through the ocean at high speeds
- On reaching a gently sloping coastline the waves slow and compress upwards
- Waves surge ashore to cause devastation well beyond the beach

Technology that can help
1. Recorder on sea bed monitors sea pressure and activity every 15 mins – an unusual result triggers readings every 15 secs
2. Surface buoy monitors upper level conditions and relays this plus data from seabed sensors to satellite
3. Satellite receives data and relays it to ground stations

12 Report your group's ideas to the class. Answer their questions.

PROJECT » 13 Find out about an important test in your industry. Get information about:
- the objectives of the test
- the test procedure
- results

14 Give a short talk about this to the class.

11 Design

1 Working robots

START HERE » 1 Brainstorm with a partner. What kind of working robots have you heard about? What jobs do they do?

SCANNING » 2 Practise your speed reading. Look for the information you need on the SPEED SEARCH pages (118–119). Try to be the first to complete the task.

Task: Answer these questions about industrial robots.
- What percentage of the world's robots work in car assembly?
- Which five countries have about three-quarters of the world's robots?
- How far did the Mars robot *Opportunity* travel on Mars?

LISTENING » 3 Look at these robots. What do you think they do?

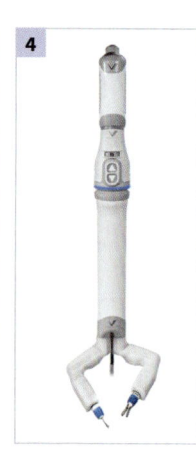

4 🔊 11.1 Listen to these interviews with participants at an industrial robot convention. Which robots (in 3) are the speakers looking at?

5 Listen again. The participants mention some strengths and weaknesses of the robots they use, and suggest some improvements. Complete the form.

ROBOT USER SURVEY FORM			
USER # 1	OCCUPATION: Construction engineer	ROBOT NAME:	SnakeBot
Function of robot	It brings		
Strength(s)	1.	2.	
Weakness(es)			
Improvement(s)			
USER # 2	OCCUPATION: Emergency first responder	ROBOT NAME:	Rescue Robot
Function of robot			
Strength(s)	1.	2.	
Weakness(es)			
Improvement(s)			

6 🔊 11.2 Listen to part of the first interview again. Then complete this dialogue with the correct form of the words in the box.

> advantage   disadvantage   drawback   suggest   could   should   that   strength   weakness   would (x2)   if

I = Interviewer; P1 = Participant 1

I: So what are the (1) **advantages** of the SnakeBot?
P1: Well, its main (2) _____ is that it can twist around things like girders, pipes and scaffolding.
I: Excellent. So, would you say that it has any (3) _____, or (4) _____?
P1: Yes, its main (5) _____ is (6) _____ I have to give it commands from my tablet.
I: So, in the future, how (7) _____ you (8) _____ that it (9) _____ be improved?
P1: Well, it (10) _____ be great (11) _____ the designers (12) _____ add voice-activation.

SPEAKING »

7 Tell the class about the strengths and weaknesses of some of these products and/or any others you have problems with. Suggest improvements.

computer keyboard, swimming goggles, earphones, sunglasses, smartphone, digital camera, TV remote

8 Work in pairs, A and B.

Student A.
1 You are conducting a survey of people who use robots in their work. Ask B about their robot and make notes on the form.
2 Turn to page 113 for information about you and your robot. Identify the correct picture in 3. Answer B's questions.

Student B.
1 Turn to page 116 for information about you and your robot. Identify the correct picture in 3. Answer A's questions.
2 You are conducting a survey of people who use robots in their work. Ask A about their robot and make notes on the form.

ROBOT USER SURVEY	
Occupation of user	
Name of robot	
Function of robot	
Frequency of use	
Specifications of robot	
How it works	
Strength(s)	
Weakness(es)	
Suggested improvement(s)	

WRITING »

9 Write a short report about your partner's robot and how it could be improved. Use the information from the form.

2 Eco-friendly planes

START HERE »

1. What do you know about the forces which act on a plane?
   - Label the diagram with these words: *thrust, weight, drag, lift*.
   - Explain the role of *the engine, gravity, friction* and *shape of wing* in these forces.

2. Discuss with a partner. Look at the photos. What effect will the forces of thrust, weight, drag and lift have on these types of planes?

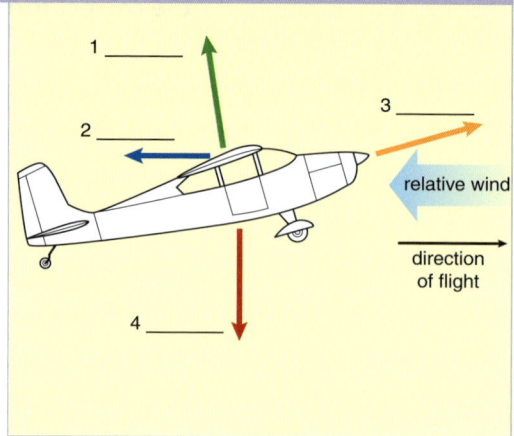

READING »

3. Read this magazine article and write the plane design numbers in the gaps.

Eco-friendly planes of the future

Engineers and designers continue to research how to make air travel less harmful to the environment. Here are four designs for future passenger planes. The aim of all the designs is to reduce drag (caused by friction of the wing against the air) so that they consume less fuel and emit less greenhouse gas.

Design (1) _____ uses liquid hydrogen as fuel for combustion with oxygen. The body is narrow and the wings curve backwards at the tip. This shape is designed to reduce drag. Two hybrid-hydrogen turbofan engines on the wings provide thrust. The storage tanks for the liquid hydrogen are located towards the rear of the plane. The aircraft can carry up to 200 passengers and has a cruising speed of 828 km/h.

Design (2) _____ has a narrow body and uses diagonal struts (or braces) to support the wings. The wings are on the top of the fuselage and the struts stretch from the bottom of the fuselage. The wings are thinner and longer than those on most narrow-body aircraft today. This reduces drag and therefore allows the plane to fly high and fast, needing less thrust from the engines and so consuming almost 10% less fuel. There are plans to use hydrogen as the fuel, which emits only water vapour and can be quieter than other fuels.

Design (3) _____ re-uses a technology from the past: propellers. The three propellers, located at the rear of the plane, are powered by electric motors. The wings are long, situated at the rear of the fuselage, and have large wingtips pointing upwards. Although propellers can be more noisy than current engines, they reduce wing drag, although flight times are about 20% longer than in today's jet airliners. This will be less of a problem over short or medium distances.

Design (4) _____ combines the wings and fuselage into a single, flat, triangular structure: it is basically a giant wing with no fuselage. Windows for passengers can be located along the sides of the wing. Two engines are placed at the rear, next to the two vertical stabilisers. As a result, the airflow is smooth over the whole plane, drag is lower and less thrust is needed from the motors. Therefore, fuel consumption is about 20% lower than in other designs. The plane is lightweight and produces less noise than normal airliners. Its flat body will need extra pressure inside to resist air pressure outside.

Design A — Boeing Transonic Truss-Braced Wing

Design B — Airbus ZEROe Turbofan

Design C — Airbus MAVERIC

Design D — HER0 Zero Emissions Airplane

4 The designers of the planes in 3 worked from the design brief below. Discuss with your partner and choose:

- the best design (the one closest to the design brief)
- the worst design (the one furthest from the design brief)

Design brief for new passenger plane

1 The need
Environmental issues are very important today. Global warming and non-renewable energy resources are major problems. It is necessary to design aeroplanes which will (a) use less fuel and (b) emit less greenhouse gas into the atmosphere. In addition, (c) noise pollution has to be reduced.

2 Problems with current designs
Aeroplanes today have a number of design weaknesses. The shape of wings and fuselages create friction (or drag), so that air does not flow smoothly over them. In addition, wings have to be strong and as a result they are very heavy. This results in more engine thrust, more fuel consumption and more carbon emissions. Another problem is that engine noise is high.

3 Requirements for new design
Design a new plane which will consume approximately 20% less fuel.

The plane should be capable of long-haul flights carrying at least 200 passengers at today's speeds. The shape and design of the new wing and/or fuselage needs to allow air to flow more smoothly. As a result, engine thrust and drag must be much lower than in current designs.

The wingspan should be longer, but fewer materials must be used and the wing must be lighter than in current planes.

The shape of the fuselage can be changed, but it must remain cylindrical so that it is pressure-resistant for passenger safety. Current noise levels must not be increased.

TASK »

5 Work in small groups. Follow your group's design brief to design an improved product. Draw a diagram and write a description. Include this information. You can add more features.

- function
- shape and appearance
- main parts
- dimensions
- materials and properties
- operation (how it works)
- cost
- method of manufacture
- safety features

Group A: Your design brief is on page 111.
Group B: Your design brief is on page 113.
Group C: Your design brief is on page 114.
Group D: Your design brief is on page 116.

6 Present your new design to the class.

7 Listen to the presentations by the other group(s).

- Does their design meet the brief? Tell them why/why not.
- Tell them the advantages and disadvantages of their design.

3 Traction kites

START HERE » 1 What problems does this design help to solve?

LISTENING » 2 🔊 11.3 Listen to this designer giving a presentation about the traction kite. Put her index card notes into the correct order by numbering them 1–12.

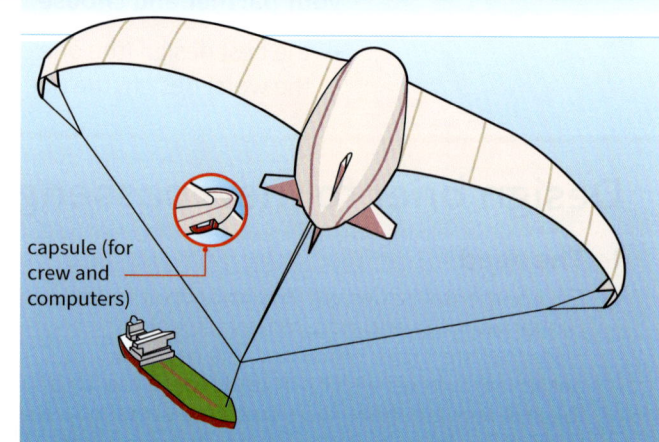
capsule (for crew and computers)

A
Materials and properties
Kite: made of polyester.
Properties: tough, flexible, lightweight, high tensile strength, low friction. ☐

B
Advantages
Wind power a renewable source.
Ships use 35% less fuel on voyage.
Carbon emissions are reduced.
Less expensive for ship owners. ☐

C
Problem
Other designs use mast and sail fixed permanently to a ship.
This is very expensive. ☐

D
The kite catches the wind.
Kite pulls ship with 6000 hp.
When wind direction changes, kite is untied from ship and travels to another client ship. ☐

E
Parts and functions
Kite has two large sails.
Sails attached to large oval balloon.
Balloon filled with helium. ☐

F
Operation
Kite crew steer kite to client ship.
They drop cable down to ship.
Ship's crew attach cable to front of ship. ☐

G
Sensors on sails detect air pressure and air speed and send data to the computers. Computers control speed and direction.
Kite connected to client ship using strong cable. ☐

H
Need
Cargo ships weigh tens of thousands of tons.
Diesel oil non-renewable and expensive.
Need to use less oil, therefore use wind energy by means of sails. ☐

I
Design brief
To design a traction kite
(a) strong enough to pull a large cargo ship through water and
(b) removeable from ship when there is no wind. ☐

G
Greet audience (don't forget!)
Objective of presentation
To tell audience about new traction kite for cargo ships and supertankers. ☐

H
Small capsule suspended from balloon. Capsule contains a 3-man crew and computers. ☐

I
Dimensions
Wingspan: 120 m.
Area of sail: 5000 m².
Altitude: 300 m above sea level. ☐

88 11 Design

3 The speaker introduces each section using signpost phrases and questions. Complete the phrases. Use the words in the box once only.

> aim brings finally look let's mention move need problem start talk turn

Speaker's headings	Speaker's words
Greeting	Good morning, everyone, and thanks for coming.
Objective	Signpost: The (1) _____ of this short presentation is to tell you about our new traction kite.
Need	Signpost: I'd like to (2) _____ by asking a question. Question: *Why do we* (3) _____ *a traction kite?*
Problem	Question: *So, what is the* (4) _____ *with other designs for sails?*
Design brief	Signpost: And that (5) _____ me to our design brief.
Materials and properties	Signpost: Now, let's (6) _____ on to materials. Question: *What is the traction kite made of?* Question: *And what are the properties of the materials?*
Parts and functions	Signpost: Right, so now (7) _____ look at the main parts of the traction kite and their function.
Dimensions	Question: *So, how large is this kite?* Question: *And how high does it fly?* Signpost: Let's (8) _____ at some dimensions.
Operation	Signpost: All right, now let's (9) _____ to the operation of the kite. Question: *How does it work?*
Advantages	Signpost: And (10) _____, I'd like to (11) _____ some of the advantages of the traction kite.

4 Listen again to the presentation. Check your answers to 3.

SPEAKING »

5 Make short presentations based on these sets of notes. Use signpost phrases or questions to signal when you move to the next point.

GREETING

AIM: describe ePad (Wi-Fi model)

SIZE & WEIGHT: 250 x 174 x 7.5 mm; display 10.2 inches diagonal; retina; weight 487 g

COLOURS: silver; space grey

BUTTONS/CONNECTORS: home + ID sensor; headphone jack; smart connector; on/off + sleep/wake

CAPACITY: two models: 64 GB; 256 GB

CAMERA: 8MP wide camera; digital zoom up to 5x; panorama up to 43MP

ACCESSORIES: USB-C cable; 20W USB-C power adapter

THANKS

GREETING

OBJECTIVE: talk about ePhone
DIMENSIONS: 152 × 69 × 7.8 mm
WEIGHT: 163 G
SCREEN SIZE & REFRESH RATE:
6.2 inches; 120 Hz
STORAGE: 128 GB
BATTERY: 12–14 hours between charges
(= 'all day'); charging speed: 15W wireless
CAMERAS: three cameras at rear: (1) 16 MP
(PDAF); (2) 8 MP (ultra-wide); (3) 2 MP
(macro) for close-up photography; plus one
camera at front: 2 MP
BIOMETRICS: fingerprint (touch)
CONNECTIVITY & FEATURES: Bluetooth
5.0; 802.11 a, b, g, n, ac, dual-band; Wi-Fi
Direct, Hotspot; USB-C (reversible)

THANKS

12 Innovation

1 Zero emission

A hydrogen fuel cell test car

START HERE »

1 Look at the car in the photo. What kind of fuel does it use?

2 Work with a partner. Discuss these questions.
- How does the car in 1 work?
- Is it good for the environment? Why?/Why not?

TASK »

3 The power system in the car in 1 combines two different technologies – fuel cells and capacitors. Work in pairs. Find out about them.

Student A: Find out about hydrogen fuel cells on page 115.

Student B: Find out about capacitors on page 117.

4 Explain to your partner how your technology works.

5 Join up with other pairs to work in small groups. Decide how the two technologies work together in the car in 1.

6 Explain your group's ideas to the class.

WRITING »

7 You are a TV journalist. You are going to interview the designer of a car called the Hydro-X, using these notes. Write questions to ask the designer.

> New type of car needed? Why? To protect environment? Electric vehicles?
> Problems with current electric vehicles? Solution?
> New Hydro-X car ... Cruising speed (km/h)? Range (km)? Acceleration? Emissions?
> Hydro-X ... Refuelling time? Weight of battery? Emissions?
> Components ... Fuel cell ... Power output (kW)? Location (front/rear/underneath)? Why located there?
> Motor ... Location? Output (kW)? Torque?
> Control unit ... Function/Purpose? Location?
> Ultra-capacitor ... Function? Location? Why located there? Power (V)?
> Hydrogen storage tanks ... Location? Capacity (kg)? How connected to fuel cell?
> Air pump ... Why needed? Location?

READING » 8 Read the press release and find answers to the questions you have written.

The new Hydro-X hydrogen fuel cell car

We need to protect our environment by reducing our emissions of greenhouse gases into the atmosphere. There are great hopes for the future that electric vehicles will help. However, many electric vehicles are powered by heavy batteries with long recharging times.

There is a technology that can solve this problem: the hydrogen fuel cell electric vehicle (FCEV). Many traffic experts believe that FCEVs are the way of the future.

Our new Hydro-X FCEV has a stack of 330 hydrogen fuel cells that weigh only 32 kg. This light weight is only possible because the fuel cells are not needed for acceleration. Instead, the power for rapid acceleration – from zero to 100 km/h in eight seconds – comes from the ultra-capacitor. The car can cruise at 160 km/h and has a range of 650 km. Best of all, you can refuel in less than five minutes. And its gift to the environment? It only emits a small amount of water vapour.

The fuel cell, positioned under the floor, provides a maximum output of 128 kW. The motor, mounted between the front wheels, provides high output (133 kW) and powerful torque (406 Nm). The control unit, located over the motor, controls the electrical systems. The ultra-capacitor, set behind the rear seat, delivers immediate high-output power (310 V) during startup and acceleration, and recovers the energy generated during braking. The hydrogen storage tanks, placed under the rear seat, can be filled with 5.6 kg of compressed hydrogen gas in about four minutes. The tanks are connected to the fuel cell by special pipes. The air pump, mounted directly on the motor, supplies the fuel cell with oxygen.

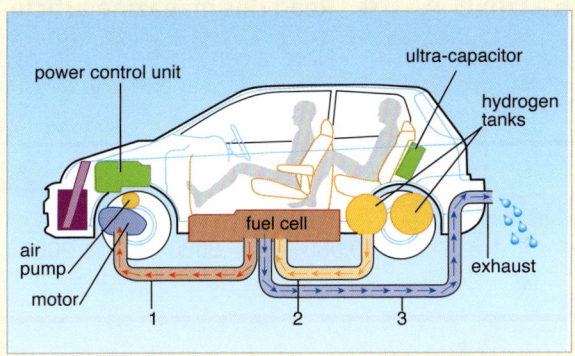

9 Complete the labels (1–3) in the diagram in 8.

> water   hydrogen   electricity

SPEAKING » 10 Roleplay the interview between the journalist and the inventor.

LANGUAGE » The words in the box can be omitted. The sentences mean the same.

- The ultra-capacitor recovers the energy [which is] generated during braking.
- The ultra-capacitor recovers the energy generated during braking.

The words in blue are an example of a reduced relative clause.

11 Underline the reduced relative clauses in these sentences.

1 The air pump, <u>mounted on the motor</u>, supplies the fuel cell with oxygen.
2 The fuel cell, positioned under the floor, provides an output of 128 kW.
3 The motor, located between the front wheels, provides high output.
4 The fuel tanks, placed under the rear seat, are filled with hydrogen.
5 The ultra-capacitor, set behind the rear seat, delivers 310 V of power.

12 Insert one of these phrases where possible in each sentence above, and in seven places in 8.

which is, which are

2 Technological change

START HERE »

1. Work in pairs. What are the ten most important tools in the history of humanity? Make a list and put them in order of importance.

   Note: the tools must be *hand-held* or *easily portable*. Do not include *simple machines* (such as levers or pulleys), *heavy machine tools* (such as hydraulic jacks) or *complex, self-running machines* (such as cars, windmills or computers).

2. Explain your list to the class. Give reasons for your group's choice.

3. Compare your list with the results of a survey on page 111. Do you agree with their list? Give reasons.

READING »

4. Read this magazine article and mark the inventions on the timeline.

   Note: a century ends in its own number. The 14th century is 1301–1400.

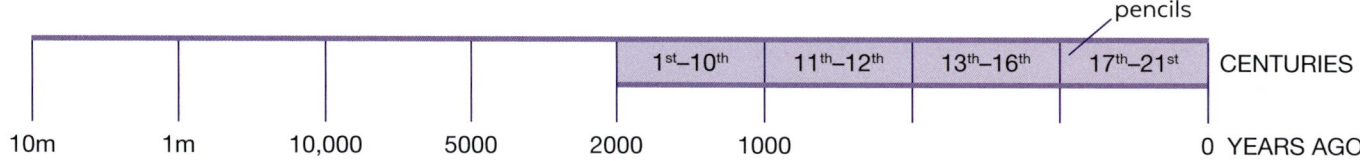

Tools through the ages

THE FIRST KNIVES were made about two and a half million years ago. They were crafted by early ancestors of modern humans. At first, sharp pieces of stone were broken off a rock, but in later times they were sharpened and straightened into blades.

The abacus is one of the first mechanical counting devices, an ancestor of today's computers. It consisted of a frame containing beads on wires. The modern abacus was designed by the Chinese around the year 1200.

The compass allowed sailors to navigate across oceans and discover new worlds. The compass was invented by the Chinese about 2200 years ago. A spoon-shaped piece of magnetic rock was balanced on a flat surface. Since it was magnetic, the handle rotated to align itself with the Earth's magnetic poles.

The first mass-produced pencils were made in Germany in 1662, which helped writing and education to develop.

The harness lets people control horses and attach them to carts. It was probably invented about 6000 years ago, when horses were first tamed and kept.

The scythe allows people to cut grass and harvest crops from the field. It consists of a long wooden shaft with handles on the end and in the middle, and a long curved blade on the other end. The blade is sharp on the inside. It was first used in Europe in the 12th century.

Glasses (or spectacles) make workers more productive and accurate, and allow people to work into old age. Mathematical calculations for a spherical lens were first made by Arab scientists in the 11th century. The first spectacles were manufactured by Italian craftsmen in the 13th century.

Saws were first used by the Egyptians more than 5000 years ago to cut both wood and stone. They were made of copper.

The first balance scales were seen in southern Mesopotamia about 9000 years ago. They consisted of two weighing pans attached to either end of a beam, which was balanced on a central pivot. They allowed merchants to calculate the exact weight of goods.

The chisel consists of a long, narrow, sharpened edge attached to a handle. It's different from a knife or axe, because it is driven by a sharp blow from a hammer or mallet. The earliest chisels were made from flint (a kind of stone) 10,000 years ago. Later, they were used by the Egyptians to carve stone for the pyramids.

VOCABULARY » 5 Do you know these simple machines? Match the pictures with the words and phrases in the box.

> cam and follower   crank and rod   gear   lever   pulley and belt   rack and pinion
> ratchet and pawl   screw   wheel and axle   wedge

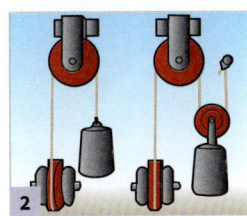
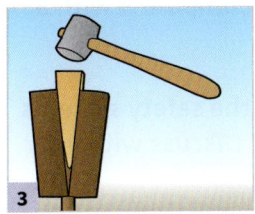
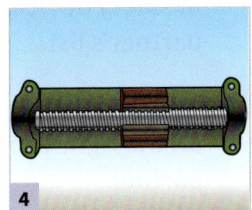
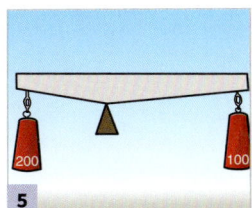
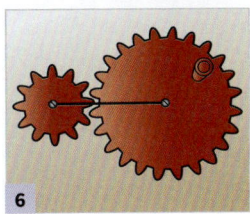

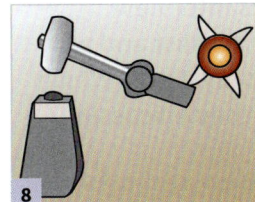

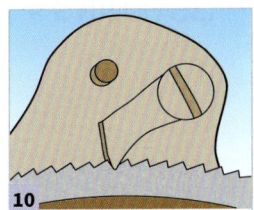

(Answers on page 114)

6 Which of these simple machines are used in your industry or technical field? How are they used? Explain to the class.

LANGUAGE » 7 Complete this article about the history of oil drilling. Use the correct form (present or past, active or passive) of the verbs in brackets.

Drilling for oil – past and present

Long ago, wells (1) <u>were dug</u> (dig) in the ground using percussion drilling. A heavy wooden cutting tool (2) _____ (suspend) by a rope from a pulley on a wooden tripod. The tool (3) _____ (pull up) by hand or steam engine, and then it (4) _____ (drop) into the hole. The rock (5) _____ (break) by the weight of the tool. The maximum depth was only about 70 metres.

Nowadays, much deeper oil wells of 700 m (6) _____ (dig) using a method called rotary drilling. A sharp drill bit (7) _____ (suspend) by a drill string from a pulley on a steel derrick. The drill bit (8) _____ (rotate) in the hole by a powerful engine. The rock (9) _____ (break) by the rotation of the drill bit.

Now there is also a new method of drilling which (10) <u>cuts</u> (cut) the rock using lasers. No cutting tool or drill bit (11) _____ (use). Instead, the rock (12) _____ (split) by beams of high-energy light. A fibre-optic cable (13) _____ (carry) the light from the lasers on the surface down the hole to a set of lenses. The lenses then (14) _____ (focus) the light to a sharp point on the rock face, which (15) _____ (cut) almost 100 times faster than by a drill bit. As a result, the cost of drilling (16) _____ (reduce) and drilling jobs (17) _____ (complete) much more quickly.

TASK » 8 Work in small groups.

- Choose an industry or work process which you know something about.
  Examples: *building, heavy lifting, fishing, mining, road-building, communications, sea or land travel, heating, lighting, pumping, irrigation*
- How was the work done in the past? How is it done now? Make notes showing the contrast between past and present.
- Explain your group's ideas to the class.

3 Vehicle safety

START HERE »

1. What car safety systems are fitted as standard in new cars? Make a list of safety devices. Compare it with a partner's list.

2. How do you think the safety systems on the right work? Discuss with your partner.

LISTENING »

3. 🔊 12.1 Listen to this interview between a radio journalist and an expert on car safety systems. Which system from 2 are they discussing?

4. Listen to the interview again. As you listen, look at the journalist's checklist. Delete any questions she does not ask.

Questions about the safety system

- name of system: _____
- name of designer: _____
- function or purpose: _____
- need: _____
- technology / principle: _____
- main parts / features: _____
- location of parts: _____
- operation / how it works: _____
- advantages: _____
- disadvantages: _____

5. Listen to the interview again and note down the main points of the expert's answers in the checklist.

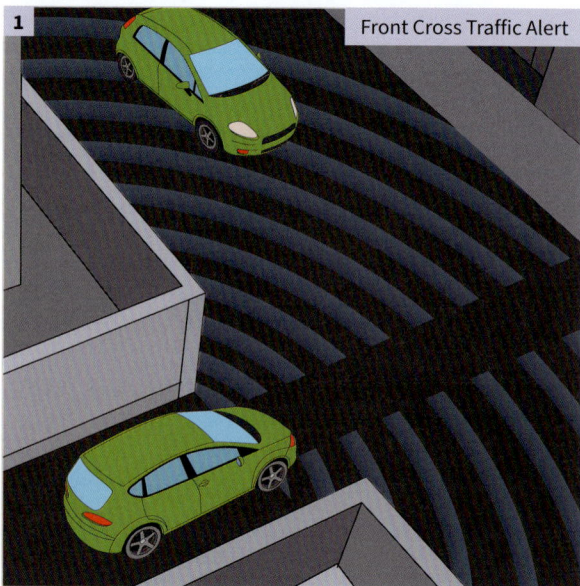

1 Front Cross Traffic Alert

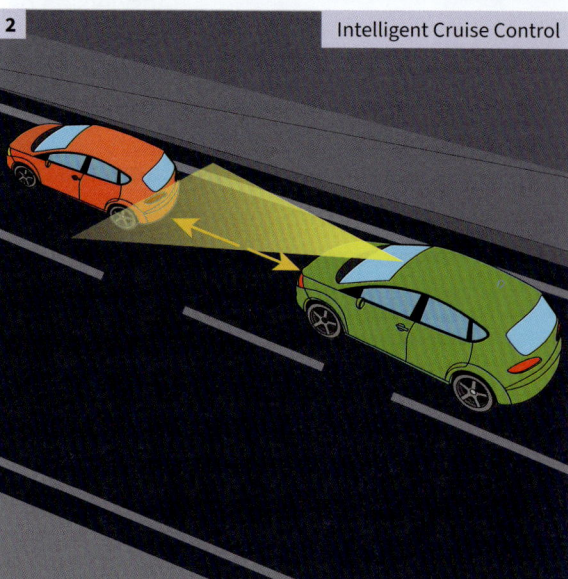

2 Intelligent Cruise Control

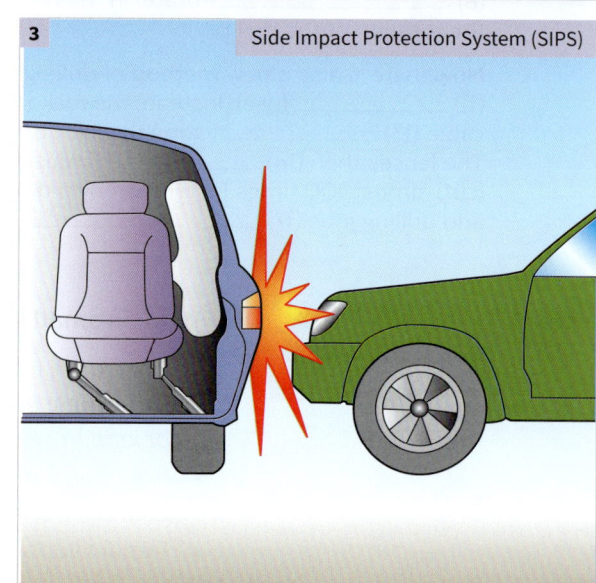

3 Side Impact Protection System (SIPS)

6 🔊 12.2 The journalist is interviewing the car safety engineer about her career. Correct the mistakes in her biodata.

MICHELA ROSSI is a design engineer at Central Motors. She gained her technician's diploma in automotive manufacture from Toulouse Technical Institute and then gained a degree in automotive engineering at the Polytechnic University of Turin. She joined Central Motors four years ago, and in that time she has designed or invented four new products with her team. She's now working on a new type of air bag for cars. She plans to continue working at Central Motors for several years and then she wants to start her own design company.

SPEAKING »

7 Work in pairs, A and B. Roleplay an interview between a journalist and a car safety engineer.

Student A: You are the radio journalist. Interview Student B about his/her career. Find out about B's, *company*, *how long in company*, *job title*, *number of inventions*, *diploma*, *degree*, *plans for future inventions*, *plans for career*.

Student B: You are a car safety engineer. You can use one of the bio-data factsheets on page 117. Alternatively, you can make some notes using similar information about yourself. Answer A's questions.

8 Find out about each other's car safety system. Take turns to roleplay the parts of a journalist and a car safety expert.

Student A: You are an expert on the Side Impact Protection System (SIPS). Read the factsheet on page 114 and refer to the diagram in 2. Answer a journalist's questions about the SIPS system.

Student B: You are an expert on the Front Cross Traffic Alert system. Read the factsheet on page 117 and refer to the diagram in 2. Answer a journalist's questions about the system.

WRITING »

9 Write a press release on your car safety system. Refer to the press release on page 91. Use these headings.

Need for this safety system
Problems with current systems
Description of the system
Technology used in system
Advantages

Main components
Location of each component
Function of each component
How the system works

TASK »

10 Work in small groups.

- Choose one of the car systems on pages 113, 115 or 116.
- Read the factsheet. Add notes giving your own ideas and opinions about the system.
- Explain the system to the rest of the group.
- Answer their questions about it.

Review Unit F

1. Write questions to get the answers in the questionnaire below.

Q 6 How _____?
Q 8 When _____?
Q 10 Are _____?
Q 11 What _____?
Q 12 What _____?
Q 13 Where _____?
Q 16 How _____?
Q 17 What _____?
Q 18 Does _____?
Q 19 How _____?

2. Work in pairs. Practise the interview. Use the questionnaire.

ROBOT USER SURVEY

1. **Age:** 18–21 ☐ 22–30 ☒ 31–45 ☐ > 46 ☐
2. **Job type:** operative ☐ technician ☐ engineer ☒ manager ☐ other _____
3. **Exact job title:** Subsea Maintenance Engineer
4. **Workplace:** factory ☐ office ☐ site ☐ laboratory ☐ other deep-water oil rig
5. **Industry:** construction ☐ electrical ☐ telecom ☐ IT ☐ biomed ☐ other oil
6. **No of years in job:** < 5 ☐ 5–10 ☒ 11–20 ☐ > 20 ☐
7. **Type of robot used:** Resident Subsea Drone
8. **Date of purchase:** eight months ago
9. **Frequency of use:** < 10% ☐ 10–25% ☐ 26–50% ☐ 51–75% ☐ > 75% ☒
10. **Using now/today?** YES ☒ NO ☐
11. **Main function/purpose:** moving ☐ detecting ☒ doing ☐ other + repairing
12. **Abilities:** walk ☐ run ☐ ride ☐ carry ☐ other swim
13. **Location of use:** On sea bed
14. **Shape:** Long, cylindrical, like an eel
15. **Approximate dimensions:** 6 m long
16. **Method of operation:** Battery-operated remote control.
17. **Advantages/strengths:** Can work in dangerous places on sea bed.
18. **Disadvantages/weaknesses/design flaws:** It has only six thrusters.
19. **Suggested improvements:** Add two more thrusters.
20. **Comparison with human:** better ☒ worse ☐

3 Match each signpost with the information which follows it.

Signpost	Information
1 First, I'd like to give you a definition of the SnakeBot. 2 OK, I've defined the device. But what is it able to do? 3 Now let's move on to the main components of the robot. 4 Right, now I'd like to talk about the function of each component. 5 OK, we've looked at its parts and what they do, so now let's look at its operation. 6 And finally, I'd like to mention its main strengths.	a) The SnakeBot has of a number of modules which consist of sensors and actuators. You can add more modules, or replace them easily. The robot also has video cameras, LED lights and lasers that can measure distance. b) A SnakeBot is basically a computer-controlled robotic device which looks and moves like a snake. c) It works like this. The controller uses a tablet to set the task, and then the SnakeBot navigates itself along the best route to achieve the task. For example, when it climbs a pole, the robot can change its own movement based on changes in the radius of the pole. d) The most important advantage of the SnakeBot is that you can control it remotely from a long distance. e) It can climb scaffolding and carry a tool to a builder at the top of a high-rise building. f) The job of the the sensors is to detect changes in the environment and send this data to the software that controls the actuators. The actuators work together to produce snake-like twisting movements to navigate the environment.

4 Complete this set of notes using a device you know about.

Aim: to talk about	(name of device)
Specifications:	(e.g. dimensions, weight, speed)
Main parts and functions:	
Materials and properties:	
Operation/How it works:	
Strengths:	
Weaknesses:	

5 Give a short talk from your notes. Use signpost phrases or questions to signal when you move to the next point in the notes.

Remember to begin your talk by welcoming the audience, and end by thanking them.

6 Complete this text. Use the present or past passive of the verbs in brackets.

Here are some examples of spinoffs from space travel. The devices (1) <u>were created</u> (create) many years ago for space programmes. But now they (2) <u>are used</u> (use) by many people in everyday life.

The smoke detector (3) _____ (make) for the Skylab space station in the 1970s to detect toxic gases. Now they (4) _____ (install) in most buildings to warn people of fire.

The CADCAM online and console program (5) _____ (invent) by NASA engineers over 20 years ago to find problems in spaceships. Now nearly all cars (6) _____ (design) using these programs.

Today, many online and console games (7) _____ (control) by means of small joysticks. In fact, joysticks (8) _____ (introduce) many years ago to control the Apollo Lunar Rover.

7 Write a description of the space elevator, using all the information. Add your own ideas and opinions.

You can use your own headings to paragraphs, or use these words in your headings: *definition, purpose, main components, function of components, specifications, dimensions, location, speed, material, properties, operation, advantages, problems.*

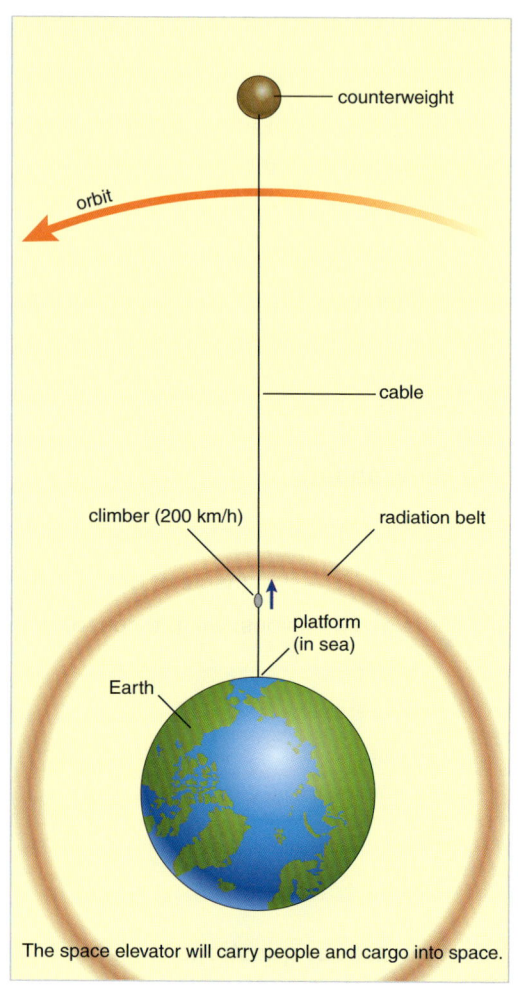

The space elevator will carry people and cargo into space.

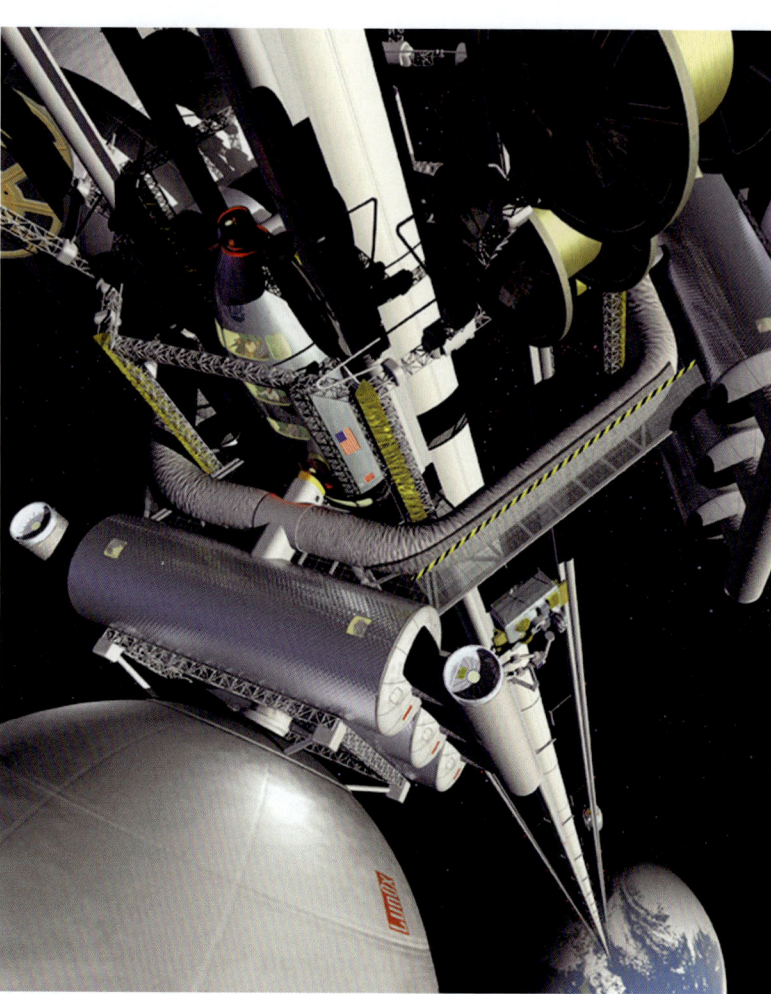

Cable for space elevator	
length	100,000 km
material	carbon nanotubes
properties	light, cheap, strong in tension
advantage	can manufacture it cheaply

Advantage: rocket propulsion not needed
Problem: radiation belt at 1000–20,000 km altitude

OPERATION

counterweight floats in zero gravity

earth rotates → platform pulls cable → counterweight tightens it

robot climber moves up cable, escapes gravity of Earth

8 Insert one of the phrases from the box in the text where possible. Use each phrase once only.

> that are   that is   which is   which was

> Intelligent Cruise Control is a car safety system invented by a team of engineers at Central Motors. It can be found in all new cars manufactured by Central Motors. It is an automatic impact-prevention system designed to maintain a safe distance between your car and the vehicle in front. It uses a laser sensor mounted on the front of the vehicle in the upper part of the windscreen.

9 Work with a partner. Discuss these inventions.

- What need or problem do they attempt to solve?
- What is their purpose? (Answers on page 116)
- What are their strengths and weaknesses?

PROJECT »

10 Work individually.

- Research the history of a key technology in your industry.
- Draw a timeline with notes of important changes in the technology.
- Write notes about the past, present and future of the technology.
- Prepare and give a short talk to the class.

11 Work in small groups.

- Choose a product that you would like to improve or re-design.
- Use the internet and/or a library to find ideas for a new design.
- Brainstorm ways to modify and improve the product. Make notes.
- Using your notes, discuss and decide the design brief.
- Write the design brief for the new product.
- Design the new product, following your group's design brief. Make sketches.
- Prepare a presentation about your new product. Draw a large visual to show the class.
- Give a group presentation about your new product. Refer to your visual during your talk.

Grammar summary

A Grammar

Present simple

Positive		
He/She	works/studies	at Oxford University.
I/You/We/They	work/study	
The water	flows	into the tank.
The electrons	flow	along the wire.

Negative				
I/We/They	do	not	work	on an oil platform.
He/She	does			

Question				
Where	do	you/they	work?	
	does	he/she		

The present simple is used to talk about
(1) regular or routine events: *Tore goes home to Norway every two weeks.*
(2) job descriptions: *The chief electrician supervises a team of four electricians.*
(3) processes: *The water flows from the tank into the solar water panel.*

Present continuous

Positive			
I	am	studying	electronics.
You/We/They	are	breaking	the safety rules.
He/She/The robot	is	cleaning	the car.

Negative				
I	am	not	studying	electronics.
You/We/They	are	not	breaking	the safety rules.
He/She/The robot	is	not	cleaning	the car.

Question			
Am	I	talking	to the manager?
Are	you/we/they	working	on the same project?
Is	he/she/the robot	wearing	a hard hat?

The present continuous is used to talk about
(1) things happening now (while the speaker is speaking): *I'm taking the wheel off now.*
(2) things happening for a limited time around now: *I'm studying electronics this year.*
(3) plans or intentions for the near future: *I'm flying home tomorrow.*

Future

will and *won't* are used to talk about things that you think are certain to happen in the future.
I won't be at the meeting. I'll be in Paris all next week. The train from London will arrive at platform 2.
The present continuous or *going to* + verb is used to talk about plans or intentions.
I'm holding a meeting next Thursday. I'm going to hold a meeting next Thursday.
to is used after verbs such as *plan, intend, want, hope.*
I want to finish this report next week. I intend to complete this project next month. I hope to do it tomorrow.

Present perfect

The present perfect uses *have/has* + past participle.

Positive			
I/You/We/They	have	repaired	the car.
He/She	has	broken	the printer.

Negative				
I/You/We/They	have	not	repaired	the car.
He/She	has	not	broken	the printer.

Question			
Have	you/they	repaired	the car?
Has	he/she	broken	the printer?

The present perfect is used to talk about events during a period of time lasting from the past right up to the present time.

You can use *for*, *since*, *just* and *yet*:
- *for* focuses on the length of a period of time: *Jan has worked in Britain for three years.* (Jan is still working in Britain.)
- *since* focuses on the starting point of a period of time: *Jan has worked in Britain since 2018.* (Jan is still working in Britain.)
- *just* emphasises that the event happened recently: *My car has just broken down.* (This happened perhaps one or two minutes before now.)
- *yet* (in questions and negatives) emphasises the period of time to the present. *Haven't you finished that job yet? He hasn't cleaned the car yet.* (The job is not done. The car is dirty.)

The present perfect isn't used with times or dates of the event.

Past simple

Positive			
I/You/We/They He/She/It	repaired	the car	yesterday.
	broke	the printer	two days ago.

Negative					
I/You/We/They He/She/It	did	not	repair	the car	yesterday.
			break	the printer	two days ago.

Question				
When	did	I/you/we/they/he/she/it	repair	the car?
			break	the printer?

The past simple is used to talk about events which happened at a specific time in the past.

You can use these time expressions with the past simple:
- *yesterday, this morning, the day before yesterday*
- *three minutes ago, two days ago, five weeks ago*
- *last week, last month, last year*
- *in 2005, on the 20th October, at 6.30*

Present perfect v past simple

Here is an example of the difference between the present perfect and the past simple. Anna has written this in her CV:

Work experience 1
Dates September 2020 to the present day
Employer Omega Studios

September 2020 to the present day is a period of time from the past to the present. Anna still works at Omega Studios, and so these questions and answers use the present perfect:

Q: *How long have you worked at Omega Studios?*
A: *I've worked at Omega from 2020 to the present day. I've worked there since 2020. I've been there for two/three/ten years.*

Anna has also written this:

Work experience 2
Dates 2017–2019
Employer Comet Electronics

2017–2019 is a period of time in the past, and so these questions and answers use the past simple:

Q: *How long did you work at Comet Electronics?*
A: *I worked at Comet from 2017 to 2019. I worked there for two years.*
Q: *When did you join the company?*
A: *I joined it in July 2017. I started there four/five/ten years ago.*

The pronoun *one*

one is used when:
- someone has already mentioned a thing
- there is a choice between two or more types of the thing
- you don't want to repeat the name of the thing.

A: *Please pass me a spanner.*
B: *Which one do you want? The long one or the short one?*

Speaker B mentions two types of spanner, but does not want to repeat the word *spanner*.

Here are some common combinations:

Which one? Which ones? This one. These ones. That one. Those ones. The red one. The other one. The one with the cover. The one without the handle.

Grammar summary 101

Present simple passive

In an active sentence, the subject is the same as the agent. The subject does the action.

Subject = Agent	Active verb	Object
400 robots	paint	the car body.
Five technicians	service	the robots.

In a passive sentence, the subject is NOT the same as the agent. The subject doesn't do the action. The agent does the action to the subject.

Subject	Passive verb		Agent
	be	Past participle	
The car body	is	painted	by 400 robots.
The robots	are	serviced	by five technicians.

The passive is often used in technical writing for two main reasons:

1. The passive can make the writing clearer:
   The coolant flows into the radiator. (ACTIVE)
   Here the fan cools it. (ACTIVE)
   ✻ *The coolant flows into the radiator.* (ACTIVE).
   Here it is cooled by the fan. (PASSIVE).

   The second pair of sentences is probably clearer than the first pair, because *the water* is the topic of both sentences. The passive allows the writer to keep *the water* as the topic of both sentences.

2. The passive helps the reader to focus on actions, because you can omit the agent:
   Robots weld the car body together. Then the robots paint the car. Next, they clean the body.
   ✻ *First, the car body is welded together. Then, it is painted. Next, it is cleaned.*

   In this description of a process, the writer is interested in the actions (*welding*, *painting* and *cleaning*). The agent (*robots*) is omitted because the reader isn't interested in it (or already knows about it).

Past simple passive

The past passive uses *was/were* + past participle.

The building work	was	completed	last month.
Three skybridges	were	built	between the two towers.

The past simple passive is often used in technical writing when talking about actions or a process in the past. The reasons for using the passive are the same as for the present simple passive.

In the examples above, the agents are omitted. The writer and reader are only interested in the actions. They already know (or they aren't interested in) who did the actions.

Modal verbs v semi-modal verbs

Modal verbs. *Must* and *should* are modal verbs. They don't take -*s* in the 3rd person. They don't use *do/does* in the question or negative.

He must wear/He should wear his helmet here.
Must/Should she wear her helmet here?
He must not/should not take off his helmet here.

Semi-modal verbs. *Have to* and *need to* are semi-modal verbs. They are like modals in meaning, but have the same form as normal verbs. They take -*s* in the 3rd person. They use *do/does* in the question or negative.
He has to/needs to wear his helmet here.
Does she have to/need to wear her helmet here?
He does not have to/does not need to wear his helmet here.

The negative forms of *have to* and *need to* have a different meaning from the negatives of *must* and *should*:

Essential	Recommended	Unnecessary
You must do it. You have to do it. You need to do it.	You should do it.	You don't have to do it. You don't need to do it.
You mustn't do it.	You shouldn't do it.	

Modal verb + passive

Must, *should*, *have to* and *need to* are often followed by passive verbs in safety rules and procedures.

Your helmet	must/should		be	worn.
	has to/needs to			
Goggles	must/should/have to/need to			
	must/should	not	be	taken off.

Non-defining relative clause

In these sentences, the clauses beginning with *which* and *who* are non-defining relative clauses.

Signals are transmitted to the satellite, which then sends the signals to Earth.

John reports to Adel, who is the training manager.

The non-defining relative clause is a useful way to join two sentences together. It can be used when the word (or words) at the end of the first sentence becomes the subject of the next sentence.

Signals are transmitted to	the satellite. The satellite	then sends the signals to Earth.
	the satellite, which	

John reports to	Adel. Adel	is the training manager.
	Adel, who	

Non-defining relative clauses don't provide part of a definition or limit the meaning of the preceding word. They simply add further information. A comma is used immediately before *which/who*.

Defining relative clause

In the sentences below, the clauses beginning with *which*, *that* and *who* are defining relative clauses. They are often used in definitions. They limit the meanings of the preceding words, e.g. the thermometer in the table below isn't any kind of instrument: it's a limited type of instrument restricted to measuring temperature.

	Defining relative clause
A thermometer is an instrument	which measures temperature.
A satellite is a man-made body	that orbits the Earth.
Inventors are people	who create new devices.

Which is used with things and *who* is used with people. In defining relative clauses, *that* can replace *which* or *who*. There is no comma immediately before *which/ who/that*.

Reduced relative clause

When the relative clause contains a passive, you can omit *which/that/who* + *is/are/was/were* without changing the meaning. The shorter relative clause is called a reduced relative clause.

Steel is an alloy	which is	made from iron ore.

Steel is an alloy *made from iron ore*.

LEDs are small lights	that are	found on many devices.

LEDs are small lights *found on many devices*.

The *Titanic* was a large ship	that was	sunk by an iceberg.

The *Titanic* was a large ship *sunk by an iceberg*.

The *Titanic* sent distress signals,	which were	picked up by the *Carpathia*.

The *Titanic* sent distress signals, *picked up by the Carpathia*.

You can reduce defining and non-defining relative clauses in this way.

Noun clause

	Noun clause	
Check Make sure/ Ensure	that	the screws are tight. your mobile is turned off.
The dial indicates The gauge tells us	that	the pressure has increased. the speed is too high.

Time clause

When often indicates that two actions happen in sequence, one immediately after the other:

When the spark plug ignites, the gases explode.

As often indicates that two actions happen simultaneously, both at the same time:

As the piston moves up, it compresses the fuel.

In practice, it's often difficult to decide if two actions are simultaneous or in rapid sequence. For this reason, *when* or *as* can sometimes be used with the same meaning:

When/As the brake pedal is pressed, the piston pushes the oil along the brake pipe.

Indirect *Wh-* question

	Noun phrase
Please tell me I need to know This instrument can show you The computer calculates	their position. your speed. the altitude of the planes.
	Indirect question
	where they are. how fast you are going. how high the planes are.

Direct questions invert the word order:
Where are they? How fast are you going?

Indirect questions don't invert the word order:
Tell me where they are. I need to know how fast you are going.

Indirect *Yes/No* question (*if/whether*)

Direct *Yes/No* questions:
Is this plastic strong? Does it break easily? Will it bend?

Indirect questions based on *Yes/No* questions:
I want to know if this plastic is strong. We want to discover whether the material breaks easily. The test will find out if the material will bend.

Noun + noun phrase

Noun + noun combinations are very common in technical English e.g:

acceleration sensors (= sensors which measure acceleration)
vehicle crash tests (= tests which crash a vehicle to measure its safety)
a side impact crash dummy (= a dummy which measures the impact from the side in a crash)

Phrasal verbs

Phrasal verbs (e.g. *take off*, *pick up*, *take away*) are composed of two parts: verb (e.g. *take*) + adverb (e.g. *off*). They use this word order:

Imperative	Present continuous	Present perfect
Take the tyres off.	*I'm taking the tyres off now.*	*I've taken the tyres off.*
Take off the tyres.	*I'm taking off the tyres now.*	*I've taken off the tyres.*
Take them off.	*I'm taking them off.*	*I've taken them off.*
Not: ~~*Take off them.*~~	Not: ~~*I'm taking off them.*~~	Not: ~~*I've taken off them.*~~

Note: phrasal verbs shouldn't be confused with verbs followed by a preposition + noun/pronoun. Here are some common examples:

We climbed up the mountain. They walked through the warehouse. The car drove off the road.

In these examples, you can change the noun into a pronoun: *We climbed up it. They walked through it. The car drove off it.*

Here *up*, *through* and *off* are prepositions (not adverbs) and must be followed by a noun or pronoun.

Comparative adjectives

The comparative form of single-syllable adjectives ends in *-er*, e.g. *longer*, *wider*.

Two-syllable adjectives ending in *-y* also end in *-er*, e.g. *noisy* → *noisier*.

Notice the spelling changes: *big* → *bigger*; *wide* → *wider*; *easy* → *easier.*

When comparing two items, use *than* after the comparative adjective, e.g. *The van is higher than the car*.

There are five irregular comparatives: *better* (*good*), *worse* (*bad*), *farther/further* (*far*), *more* and *less*.

With other adjectives of more than one syllable, use *more* + adjective, e.g. *more expensive*. Use *less* with all types of adjective, e.g. *less cheap*, *less expensive*.

Superlative adjectives

To change the comparative into the superlative form, change *-er* to *-est*, *more* to *most* and *less* to *least*, e.g. *longest*, *widest*, *biggest*, *noisiest*, *most expensive*, *least noisy*.

The is often used in front of the superlative, e.g. *The fastest car in the world*, *The noisiest of the three engines*.

There are five irregular superlatives: *best*, *worst*, *farthest/furthest*, *most* and *least*.

Gerund: linking

You can link clauses together using verb + -ing in place of and + verb.

The heat pump extracts heat from the outside air and transfers it into the building. ✖ *The heat pump extracts heat from the outside air, transferring it into the building. When a gas is compressed, it condenses and gives out heat.* ✖ *When a gas is compressed, it condenses, giving out heat.*

Past simple and past participle forms

The past participle is part of (a) the present perfect verb and (b) the passive verb. Here are some examples of verbs in this book.

Most verbs are regular. Both the past simple and the past participle end in -ed.

Be careful of the spelling changes in the words below:

Regular (ending in -ed)	
verb	past simple/past participle
activate	activated
cancel	cancelled
carry	carried
cause	caused
curve	curved
drop	dropped
fit	fitted
ignite	ignited
injure	injured
locate	located
log in	logged in
plug in	plugged in
raise	raised
receive	received
reduce	reduced
rotate	rotated
service	serviced
shape	shaped
stop	stopped
submerge	submerged
transmit	transmitted
use	used

Some verbs are irregular. The past simple and the past participle do not end in -ed.

Irregular (not ending in -ed) past simple = past participle	
verb	past simple/past participle
bend	bent
bring	brought
build	built
burn	burnt
buy	bought
cut	cut
find	found
get	got
have	had
hold	held
leave	left
let	let
lose	lost
make	made
put	put
read	read
say	said
sell	sold
send	sent
sit	sat
tell	told

Irregular (not ending in -ed) past simple ≠ past participle		
verb	past simple	past participle
become	became	become
break	broke	broken
do	did	done
drive	drove	driven
fall	fell	fallen
fly	flew	flown
go	went	gone
rise	rose	risen
run	ran	run
speak	spoke	spoken
take	took	taken
tear	tore	torn
wear	wore	worn
write	wrote	written

B Functions and notions

Method
You can talk about method (= how to do something) in these ways:

1 when the method is an action.

	Method	
The passenger activates the machine	by touching	the screen.

2 when the method is a device.

	Method	
The robot can look ahead	by using by using by means of	a camera in its head.

Questions about method: *How do you do it? How did you do it? How is it done? How was it done?*

Aim, purpose or objective
to + verb is used to talk or write about the purpose of an action.

Why do you paint the car body? To protect it from rust.
The car body is painted to protect it from rust.
The aim/purpose/objective of painting the car body is to protect it from rust.

You combine *to* with *if/whether* to state the aim or objective of a test or investigation.

Aim	of	Process	is	to	Verb	if	Phrase
The aim The purpose The objective	of	the test the investigation	is	to	find out discover	if whether	the metal bends. the plastic breaks.

Questions about aim/purpose/objective:

Why do you do it? Why did you do it? Why is this done? Why was it done? What is/was the objective/aim of doing it?

Use or function
You can talk about the use or function of a device in various ways:

Present simple
The present simple is used when you think of a machine or device itself carrying out the action, e.g. *What does the carburettor do? It mixes air and petrol.*

for + verb *-ing*
for + *-ing* are used when you think of a human agent using a tool or device, e.g. *What's this tool for? It's for hammering in nails.* This means that someone uses it to hammer in nails.

What's this (device/tool/machine) for? What do you use it for? What can you use it for? It's for producing drinking water. You use it for charging batteries. You can use it for measuring walls.

to + verb
What's this (device) designed to do? It's designed to measure high walls. It can be used to charge batteries. You (can) use it to find lost objects.

act as + noun
You use this when the function of one object is like the function of another object, e.g. *The fan of the hovercraft acts as a propeller.*

Appearance
You can describe the shape or appearance of something in these ways:

It looks like a TV transmitter.
It's shaped like a dome. It's dome-shaped. It's a dome-shaped building.
It's in the shape of a dome.
It's in the shape of an L. It's L-shaped. It's an L-shaped building.
It's in the shape of a circle/triangle/square. It's circular/triangular/square in shape.

Questions about appearance: *What shape is it? What does it look like?*

Definition

When you explain the meaning of a word or technical term, you often give a definition.

Here is one very common way of forming a definition:

The thing you are defining	be	Type	Defining relative clause	
			pronoun	function
A thermometer	is	an instrument	which	measures temperature.
A satellite	is	a man-made body	that	orbits the Earth.
Inventors	are	people	who	create new devices.

Questions about definition: *What exactly is it? How do you define it? What's the definition of …?*

Diagnosing a problem

may, *might* and *could* are used to express a possible diagnosis.
must is used to express a certain diagnosis.
may/might/could/must + be are used to talk about the present.

The file	may/might/could	be	too large.	=	It is possible that it is too large.
	must	be	too large.	=	It is certain that it is too large.

Your firewall	may/might	be	blocking	the email	= possibility
	must	be	blocking	the email	= certainty

may/might/could/must + present perfect are used to talk about the past.

You	may/might	have	broken	it.	=	It is possible that you have broken it.
	must	have	broken	it.	=	It is certain that you have broken it.

Suggesting a solution

These are ways of suggesting a solution:
- *try* + verb + *-ing*, e.g., *Try clicking on the 'undo' button.*
- *Why don't you …?*, e.g., *Why don't you click on the 'undo' button.*
- *could*, e.g., *You could click on the 'undo' button.*

Questions asking for suggestions: *What should I do? What do you suggest I do? What do you think I should do?*

Ability

Here are some ways of expressing ability and inability when talking about properties.
- *can/cannot* + active verb: *This plastic can resist tension, but it cannot resist compression.*
- *can/cannot* + passive verb: *This steel can be stretched, but it can't be compressed.*
- suffixes *-able* and *-ible* with a passive meaning: *it's breakable = it can be broken.*

Result

These words explain the result (or effect) of something
- *As a result*, *Therefore* (at the beginning of a sentence)
- *and so*, *and therefore*, *and as a result* (connecting to a previous clause)

Cause

These words explain the cause of something
- *as*, *because*, *since*

You can reverse the order of the clauses without changing the meaning:

You can touch the neutral wire without a shock, as/because/since the system is earthed.
As/Because/Since the system is earthed, you can touch the neutral wire without a shock.

Reference section

1 Abbreviations

Length
mm millimetre(s)
cm centimetre(s)
m metre(s)
km kilometre(s)

Area
mm² square millimetre(s)
m² square metre(s)
km² square kilometre(s)

Volume/Capacity
mm³ cubic millimetre(s)
cm³ cubic centimetre(s)
m³ cubic metre(s)
km³ cubic kilometre(s)
ml millilitre(s)
cl centilitre(s)
l (or L) litre(s)

Mass/Weight
mg milligram(s)
g gram(s)
kg kilogram(s)
t tonne(s)

Time
s second (also **sec.**)
min minute (also **m**, as in **rpm**)
h hour

Electricity
A ampere(s) or amp(s)
Ah ampere hour(s)
W watt(s)
kW kilowatt(s)
kWh kilowatt hour(s)
V volt(s)

Temperature
°C degree(s) Celsius
°F degree(s) Fahrenheit

Frequency
Hz hertz
kHz kilohertz
MHz megahertz
Note: **k** (kilo = thousand) is normally lower case
M (mega = million) is normally upper case
G (giga = billion) is normally upper case

Pressure
Pa pascal(s)
kPa kilopascal(s)

Force
N newton(s)
Nm newton metre(s) (a measurement of torque)

Sound level
dB decibel(s)

Speed/Rate
m/s metre(s) per second
km/s kilometre(s) per second
km/h kilometre(s) per hour (**also kph**)
rpm revolution(s) per minute
bps (heart) beats per second

Other abbreviations and units
gal gallon(s)
pt pint(s)
in inch(es)
ft foot/feet
yd yard(s)
mi mile(s) (also **m**)
mph mile(s) per hour
mpg mile(s) per gallon
gph gallon(s) per hour
psi pound(s) per square inch
g/km gallon(s) per kilometre
lb pound(s)
oz ounce(s)
cc cubic centimetre(s) (engine capacity)

Some other abbreviations used in this book

am	in the morning
AC	alternating current
approx.	approximately
cc	(document) copied to; cubic centimetres (engine capacity)
CCTV	closed-circuit TV
CD	compact disc
CD-ROM	compact disc, read-only memory
CPR	cardio-pulmonary resuscitation (a procedure for someone who has stopped breathing and has no pulse)
CV	curriculum vitae, a summary of skills, qualifications and work experience
DC	direct current
DTV	digital TV
DVD	digital video disc
e.g.	for example
enc.	enclosed (or attached) document
etc.	and so on/etcetera
FAQ	frequently asked questions
Fig.	figure
FYI	for your information
GB	gigabytes
GPS	global positioning system
hp	horse power
IC	internal combustion
i.e.	that is; in other words
IP	internet protocol (as in IP address)
IT	information technology
L/kg	litres per kilogram
LNB	low noise block (on satellite dish)
LPG	liquid petroleum gas
MB	megabytes
MOB	man overboard
n/a	not applicable
no.	number
pm	in the afternoon (or evening)
qty	quantity
ref.	reference/with reference to
TDC	top dead centre
USB	universal serial bus
VCR	video cassette recorder
v	versus; compared with (also **vs**)

2 Symbols

Mathematical and other symbols

+	plus; positive
–	minus; negative
x	times; multiplied by (also *)
÷	over; divided by (also /)
±	plus or minus
=	equals
≠	does not equal
>	(is) more than
<	(is) less than
≥	(is) more than or equal to
≤	(is) less than or equal to
.	point (decimal number)
n^2	n squared
n^3	n cubed
n^4	n to the power four
$\sqrt{n}$	the (square) root of n
#	hash; number
°	degree(s)

Mathematical operations

formula	description	instruction
x = n * 9/5 + 32	x equals n times 9 over 5, plus 32	to find x, multiply n by 9 over 5 and add 32
x = (n – 32)*5/9	x equals n minus 32, multiplied by 5 over 9	to find x, subtract 32 from n and multiply by 5 over 9

Internet symbols

@	at
.com	dot com
A-B	A hyphen B (or A dash B)
A/B	A slash B (or A forward slash B)
A\B	A back slash B
A_B	A underscore B
A:B	A colon B

3 Fractions

Examples: Ten percent of the students study electronics. Two-thirds of them study electrical engineering.

1/4	(a/one) quarter	0.25	25%
1/2	(a/one) half	0.5	50%
3/4	three-quarters	0.75	75%
1/3	a/one-third	0.33*	33.3%*
2/3	two-thirds	0.67*	66.7%*
1/5	a/one-fifth	0.2	20%
3/5	three-fifths	0.6	60%
1/10	a/one-tenth	0.1	10%
3/10	three-tenths	0.3	30%
1/8	an/one-eighth	0.125	12.5%
7/8	seven-eighths	0.875	87.5%
1/100	a/one-hundredth	0.01	1%

* approximate numbers

4 British and American English

Here are some of the words used in this book, but there are many more. You can find more at the back of *Longman Technical English Level 1*. Key the words *American British English* into an internet search engine or *Wikipedia* to find more examples.

British English	American English
analogue	analog
block of flats	apartment building
catalogue	catalog
cross roads	intersection
crude oil	petroleum
curriculum vitae/CV	résumé
first floor (*building*)	second floor
flat (*building*)	apartment
flyover (*roads*)	overpass
gauge	gage
gear lever (*cars*)	gear shift
ground floor (*building*)	first floor
hash mark (#)	number sign
indicators (*cars*)	turn signals, blinkers
jump leads (*cars*)	jumper cables
lift (*building*)	elevator
lorry	truck
motorway (*roads*)	freeway
petrol (*refined oil*)	gas, gasoline
roof rack (*cars*)	luggage rack
roundabout (*roads*)	traffic circle
sliproad (*roads*)	ramp
socket (*elec*)	jack, outlet
tap (*plumbing*)	faucet
traffic lights	stop lights
zed (letter Z)	zee

5 Emergency number

112 (International)

6 The Europass CV format

Key *Europass* into Google or another search engine.

7 Word parts

Note: sometimes the word parts have different meanings. Check new words in a dictionary.

Word part	Usual meaning	Example
aud-	hearing	audible
centi-	hundred	centimetre
ex-	out/out of	exhaust
frig-	cold	refrigerator
hydr-	water	hydro-electric
ign-	fire	ignition
inter-	between	internet
intra-	inside	intranet
kilo-	thousand	kilometre
-less	without	wireless
lubr-	oil	lubricate
-meter	measurement	thermometer
micro-	very small	micro-chip
mini-	small	minimum
multi-	many	multi-storey
non-	not	non-flammable
poly-	many	polytechnic
-proof	preventing	fireproof
re-	again, back	reboot
semi-	half	semicircle
sol-	sun	solar
sub-	under	submarine
super-	much greater	supertanker
tele-	distant	television
therm-	heat	thermal
trans-	across	transmit
tri-	three	tripod
ultra-	very much greater	ultra-capacitor
un-	not	uncheck
vis-	seeing	visible

Extra material

1 Action 2 Training

Task exercise 6 page 7

Find instructions for your job.

**How to …
change a wheel – clean a spark plug –
check the oil level**

- Put the oil filler cap on.
- Clean the spark plug.
- Take out the dipstick.
- Clean the oil off the dipstick.
- Take off the spark plug cover.
- Lift up the car.
- Take out the dipstick again.
- Loosen the spark plug.
- Check the oil level.
- Lower the car.
- Loosen the wheel nuts.
- Place a jack under the car.
- Tighten the wheel nuts.
- Take off the oil filler cap.
- Put back the dipstick.
- Switch off the engine.
- Replace the spark plug in the socket.
- Add some oil (if necessary).
- Tighten the oil filler cap.
- Put the new wheel on.
- Remove the spark plug from the socket.
- Take away the jack.
- Put on the wheel nuts.
- Tighten the spark plug.
- Replace the spark plug cover.
- Take off the wheel nuts.
- Take off the old wheel.

3 Comparison 3 Equipment

Task exercise 6 page 25

Student A

You think that the Land Rover Defender is the best choice for the oil rig team. Study this information and then try to persuade your colleagues to choose this car.

Criteria	Land Rover Defender
Height	1969 mm
Passengers	9
Price	£53,260
Engine size	2.9 litre
Towing power	3500 kg
Ground clearance	226 mm
Max speed	117 km/h
Fuel consumption	7.8 km/L
Wheelbase	2587 mm
Tank	89 L

11 Design 2 Eco-friendly planes

Task exercise 4 page 87

Group A's design brief

> You work for an international aid agency and you specialise in appropriate technology for poor rural areas in developing countries.
>
> Your brief is to design a simple hydro-electric power system for use in small villages. The system should be able to provide enough electricity for a group of five to eight houses using a small stream flowing down a hill of about five metres with a 25-degree slope. The parts should be very inexpensive.

12 Innovation 2 Technological change

Start here exercise 3 page 92

The top ten tools of all time, according to a survey of 3000 people:

1 knife, 2 abacus, 3 compass, 4 pencil, 5 harness, 6 scythe, 7 rifle, 8 sword, 9 glasses, 10 saw

6 Procedures 1 Safety

Task exercise 7 page 43

Student A

Work with Student B. Put all the notes together in the best order and under the correct headings. There are three procedures. Each procedure has eight steps.

- Turn off any ignition sources.
- Close all the doors behind you.
- Stay with person until emergency services arrive.
- Switch off the electricity.
- If the person is not breathing, start artificial respiration.
- Cover the person with a blanket and keep them warm.
- Leave the building by the safest route.
- Lifts must not be used.
- Evacuate the workroom and close the door behind you.
- Call Chemical Safety department.
- Call 999 to evacuate injured persons.
- Report to the assembly point.

6 Procedures 3 Directions

Speaking exercise 5 page 47

Student A

1. Student B wants to go to these places:
   - the Student Centre.
   - the Cinema.

   You are on the phone. Find out where B is now, and give directions from there. (Don't tell B that the Student Centre is point 8 on the map and that the Cinema is point 1 on the map.)

2. You want to go to these places:
   - From the North Campus entrance (E2) to the Computer Centre.
   - From the South Campus entrance (E1) to the Aeronautics Department.

   Ask Student B for directions on the phone.

REVIEW UNIT C

Exercise 10 page 51

Student A's object

Describe this object to Student B. Then check B's drawing. Does it look like your object?

8 Energy 1 Wave power

Task exercise 8 page 59

Background notes for Group 1

Read the notes about this system and prepare a presentation about it.

WAVE ENERGY BUOY

DEFINITION: device / wave energy → electricity

MAIN COMPONENTS: copper coil, magnetic shaft, fibreglass container, cable

LOCATION: copper coil in buoy floats on sea surface; magnetic shaft attached by cable to seabed

MAIN SPECIFICATIONS: buoy 4 m (H); 30 m above seabed; 30 m between each buoy; 1.5–3 km from shore; 100 kW power

OPERATION: wave oscillates → magnetic shaft / reciprocate (explain to listeners: this means 'move up and down') → shaft / move / through copper coil → induce / electric current

BENEFITS: wave energy v wind energy? more reliable; renewable; no fossil fuels

PROBLEM: about 500 buoys needed; could damage ships, fish

10 Forces 3 Results

Start here exercise 1 page 78

Answers:

1 unshocked, 2 shocked, 3 unshocked, 4 both shocked, 5 shocked, 6 top unshocked; bottom shocked

3 Comparison 3 Equipment

Task exercise 6 page 25

Student B

You think that the Jeep Grand Cherokee is the best choice for the oil rig team. Study this information and then try to persuade your colleagues to choose this car.

Criteria	Jeep Grand Cherokee
Height	1781 mm
Passengers	6
Price	£37,360
Engine size	3.6 litre
Towing power	3500 kg
Ground clearance	218 mm
Max speed	206 km/h
Fuel consumption	13 km/L
Wheelbase	2915 mm
Tank	93 L

11 Design 2 Eco-friendly planes

Task exercise 4 page 87

Group B's design brief

> Driving to shops is bad for the environment and for the shopper's health. But it's difficult to do shopping on foot or cycle because of the weight and volume of shopping and the distance from most shops. Most of the shopping trolleys for sale today are not very useful or attractive. There's a need for a 'shopping trolley' that would be strong, carry a reasonable amount of shopping and be attractive for young people to use. Design a trolley either (a) for pushing on foot or (b) for towing by bicycle.

12 Innovation 3 Vehicle safety

Task exercise 10 page 95

> **FACTSHEET: Rear-seat entertainment system**
> - allows rear-seat passengers to view high-res video, play games, etc
> - a screen drops down from the ceiling behind the front seats
> - screen sizes 10–19 inches
> - remote controls, wireless headphones and video-game controls
> - HDMI inputs, USB, microSD card ports, Android operating system

11 Design 1 Working robots

Speaking exercise 8 page 85

Student A

1 Ask Student B about their robot and make notes.
2 Read the information below and answer Student B's questions.

> I'm a maintenance engineer on a deep-water oil rig. I use the Resident Subsea Drone to inspect and repair damaged pipelines on the sea bed. I use it for about 80% of my work. It's 6 m long and shaped like an eel. It has sensors and cameras at each end. It can 'live' under water at depths up to 500 m for six months without being brought up to the surface. It is self-propelling and doesn't need a power cable. It can travel 20 km along the sea bed before you have to recharge it. Main advantages: first, it can work on the sea bed in places which are too difficult or dangerous for a human diver; second, it is autonomous – you don't need to control every movement. Disadvantage: my model only has six thrusters – this could be a problem if some thrusters develop faults. I suggest the next model should have eight thrusters.

5 Descriptions 3 Definitions

Start here exercise 1 page 40

Answers: The four ideas were all successful in the TV show, *The Dragons' Den*.

6 Procedures 3 Directions
Speaking exercise 5 page 47

Student B

1 You want to go to these places:
   - From the North Campus entrance (E2) to the Student Centre.
   - From the South Campus entrance (E1) to the Cinema.

   Ask Student A for directions on the phone.

2 Student A wants to go to these places:
   - the Computer Centre.
   - the Aeronautics Department.

   You're on the phone. Find out where A is now, and give directions from there. (Don't tell A that the Computer Centre is point 7 on the map and that the Aeronautics Department is point 5 on the map.)

8 Energy 1 Wave power
Task exercise 8 page 59

Background notes for Group 2

Read the notes about this system and prepare a presentation about it.

WAVE POWER STATION

DEFINITION: device / convert energy from waves → electrical power
MAIN COMPONENTS: air chamber, turbine, generator, valves
LOCATION: fixed to the seabed; close to shore
MAIN SPECIFICATIONS: 35 m length × 35 m width; 485 tonnes weight; made of steel; 200 m from shore
OPERATION: wave enters chamber → water rises and falls in chamber → water forces air in and out of hole → moving air makes turbine rotate → turbine turns generator
BENEFITS: free energy; no fuel needed; no waste produced; not expensive to operate
PROBLEMS: noisy; must be able to resist rough weather

---

11 Design 2 Eco-friendly planes
Task exercise 4 page 87

Group C's design brief

> Your client has bought an old building and wants to make it into a hotel. But there is a small river along the front. The client wants you to design a small bridge to allow pedestrians to cross the river to the hotel. The river is 300 cm wide and 150 cm deep. The bridge must be able to support a maximum of five people at a time and be wide enough for three people standing side by side. The bridge should be accessible for pushchairs and wheelchair users so must not have steps. The surface of the bridge should be non-slip in all weather conditions. There should also be a safety device, such as a handrail, to stop people falling into the river. It should be as cheap as possible and maintenance (e.g. resurfacing or painting) should be minimal and easily completed by a non-expert.

12 Innovation 3 Vehicle safety
Speaking exercise 8 page 95

Student A

FACTSHEET: the Side Impact Protection System (SIPS)

- it cushions and protects the heads of driver and passengers in a car crash
- main parts: sensors, airbags, seat-moving mechanism
- seat-moving mechanism is located below the seats
- the airbags are located above all the side windows of the vehicle
- when sensors detect an impact, they activate the airbags
- the airbags inflate in a fraction of a second and cover the side windows
- then they deflate a few seconds later
- meanwhile, the seat is moved away from the impact danger
- sensors can detect the different sizes and weights of occupants, can detect whether seat belt is on and can detect exact location of passenger

---

12 Innovation 2 Technological change
Vocabulary exercise 5 page 93

Answers:

1 wheel and axle, 2 pulley and belt, 3 wedge, 4 screw, 5 lever, 6 gear, 7 rack and pinion, 8 cam and follower, 9 crank and rod, 10 ratchet and pawl

3 Comparison 3 Equipment

Task exercise 6 page 25

Student C

You think that the Toyota Land Cruiser is the best choice for the oil rig team. Study this information and then try to persuade your colleagues to choose this car.

Criteria	Toyota Land Cruiser
Height	1835 mm
Passengers	6
Price	£40,320
Engine size	2.8 litre
Towing power	3000 kg
Ground clearance	215 mm
Max speed	108 km/h
Fuel consumption	12.5 km/L
Wheelbase	2790 mm
Tank	87 L

12 Innovation 3 Vehicle safety

Task exercise 10 page 95

FACTSHEET: Traction control

- prevents tyres from skidding on slippery surfaces
- sensors detect if wheels receiving power have lost traction
- sensors are mounted on drive wheels
- system automatically presses the brake many times per second to those wheels
- system also reduces engine power to wheels that are slipping

12 Innovation 1 Zero emission

Task exercise 3 page 90

Student A

Find out about hydrogen fuel cells.

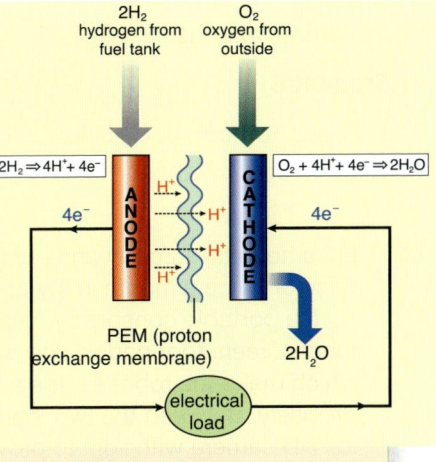

FACTSHEET: the hydrogen fuel cell

- purpose of fuel cell: to generate energy from hydrogen and oxygen
- it combines hydrogen (stored in the car's fuel tank) with oxygen (from the air outside)
- it consists of two electrodes
- negative electrode (anode) is separated from the positive one (cathode) by a proton exchange membrane (PEM) made of a special polymer
- PEM lets protons pass through it, but does not let electrons through it
- a cable connects the electrodes to an external circuit
- at anode, hydrogen splits into protons and electrons
- protons go through PEM to cathode
- electrons flow round external circuit; electricity powers the car
- at cathode, hydrogen is combined with oxygen; this produces water vapour (exhaust)

REVIEW UNIT C

Exercise 6 page 49

Answers:

from top to bottom: for measuring air pollution; for cutting a hollow tube or pipe made of metal; for recording all the data and sounds that occur during a flight; for measuring sound levels.

Exercise 10 page 51

Student B's object

Describe this object to Student A. Then check A's drawing. Does it look like your object?

5 Descriptions 2 Appearance

Start here exercise 1 page 38

Answers:

- A Plaza of the Three Powers, Brasilia, Brazil
- B Guggenheim Museum, Bilbao, Spain
- C Central Chinese Television (CCTV) Tower in Beijing, China
- D Oriental Pearl Tower, Shanghai, China

11 Design 1 Working robots

Speaking exercise 8 page 85

Student B

1 Read the information below and answer Student A's questions.
2 Ask Student A about their robot and make notes.

I'm a hospital surgeon and I use Robo Surgeon once or twice a month in my operations. I control it from a portable console by means of a monitor and touchscreen, foot pedals and pistol-grip handles, which make the robot's arms and hands move very precisely. Between the two 'hands' there is a flex-tip full HD camera with light to provide a full view of the surgical field. The main strength of this robotic system is that it is portable and can easily be moved from room to room. Another advantage is that it can carry out complex minimally invasive surgery using a simple handheld device. There is no major weakness in the design, except that it may need some adaptation for use in remote emergency situations. I would therefore suggest stronger dust-proof, heat-proof and waterproof coverings and containers for transportation.

11 Design 2 Eco-friendly planes

Task exercise 4 page 87

Group D's design brief

Rubber car tyres are the weak link in driving safety. It's impossible to prevent punctures 100% because any air-filled rubber container can be burst by a sharp enough object. Your brief is to design an airless tyre. It must have the same properties as a normal air-filled rubber tyre, that is, it must be flexible, deformable and elastic, it must protect the car and passengers against bumps in the road, it must have strong braking power and it must provide a smooth ride. And it has to be durable, safe and puncture-resistant.

12 Innovation 3 Vehicle safety

Task exercise 10 page 95

FACTSHEET: Night-vision assist

- allows driver to see people, animals or trees in the dark
- operates up to 350 m ahead
- uses thermal-imaging cameras
- cameras are mounted on front of car at bottom
- camera detects object
- image is shown on display on dashboard

8 Energy 1 Wave power

Task exercise 8 page 59

Background notes for Group 3

Read the notes about this system and prepare a presentation about it.

WAVEROLLER

DEFINITION: device / change / wave energy → electricity
MAIN COMPONENTS: base plate, moving plate, piston pump, hydraulic pipes, turbine, generator
LOCATION: base plate fixed to seabed; hydraulic pipes on sea bed; turbine and generator on shore
MAIN SPECIFICATIONS: moving plate approx. 1 m x 1 m; depth 7–15 m below sea surface; each plate produces 13 kW power
OPERATION: waves move forward and backward along sea bed → plate oscillates → pistons move in reciprocating motion → turbine rotates → generator produces electricity
BENEFITS: WaveRoller invisible because on sea bed; no noise; does not interfere with ships

REVIEW UNIT F

Exercise 9 page 99

Answers:

A This is a 3D food printer. Experts believe that the technology will decrease food waste, cut production costs and reduce global warming. 3D-printed meat could reduce our reliance on animal farming.

B The Helios solar-powered plane in the photograph was the prototype for AeroVironment's Sunglider, a remotely powered solar aircraft. Solar batteries power the aircraft during the day and collect and store energy for use at night.

C Shared electric scooters started around 2017 and have now grown into a global multi-billion dollar business. You install the mobile app from the provider and locate vehicles near you. Scan the QR code on the scooter, ride from A to B, park the scooter and stop the ride in the app.

D Electric vehicle (EV) charging lanes carry an electromagnetic field that transmits energy to the car's battery. Drivers get the power they need while their vehicles are moving. The technology means that EVs could have much smaller and lighter batteries.

3 Comparison 3 Equipment

Task exercise 6 page 25

Student D

You think that the Mitsubishi Shogun Sport is the best choice for the oil rig team. Study this information and then try to persuade your colleagues to choose this car.

Criteria	Mitsubishi Shogun Sport
Height	1805 mm
Passengers	6
Price	£37,775
Engine size	2.5 litre
Towing power	3100 kg
Ground clearance	218 mm
Max speed	180 km/h
Fuel consumption	15.8 km/L
Wheelbase	2800 mm
Tank	68 L

12 Innovation 3 Vehicle safety

Speaking exercise 8 page 95

Student B

> **FACTSHEET: Front Cross Traffic Alert**
>
> - system uses radar on the front and sides
> - detects crossing vehicles and bicycles
> - detects up to 50 m ahead
> - a heads-up display shows other vehicle's position
> - acts 2-4 seconds before traffic crosses
> - if driver continues, audio alerts sound
> - very useful in fast traffic and at night

12 Innovation 3 Vehicle safety

Speaking exercise 7 page 95

Student B

Choose one of these bio-data factsheets, or use your own bio-data.

> **BIO-DATA OF MARTIN NELSON**
>
> Martin Nelson is an innovation engineer at MotorSpace Company. He gained his diploma in automotive technology at Berlin Polytechnic and then a degree in automotive engineering at Poznan Technological University. He joined MotorSpace six years ago and in that time he's designed or invented ten new products, including a new Side Impact Protection System. He's now working on a new night-vision system for cars. He plans to start his own company next year.
>
> **BIO-DATA OF DANA BRUN**
>
> Dana Brun is a senior design engineer at Innovations Inc. After obtaining her diploma in automotive design at Lyons Technical Institute, she went on to gain her degree in systems engineering at Milan University. She's worked at Innovations for four years, during which time she's invented more than eight safety systems for cars, including a new Rear Obstacle Warning System. She's now planning to design a skid control system. She intends to stay at Innovations for at least two more years.

12 Innovation 1 Zero emission

Task exercise 3 page 90

Student B

Find out about capacitors.

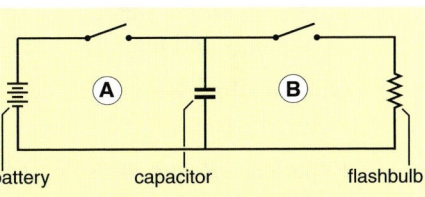

Circuit A : charges the capacitor
Circuit B : discharges the capacitor and makes the flashbulb light up for a short time

> **FACTSHEET: the capacitor**
>
> - purpose of capacitor: to provide large amount of energy for a short time
> - consists of two metal plates separated by a non-conductive material (example: plastic)
> - circuit A: close switch → battery sends current to the capacitor
> - capacitor holds the electrical charge, like a battery
> - circuit B: close switch → capacitor sends current to flashbulb in camera
> - capacitor v battery: what's the difference?
> - capacitor sends its complete electric charge in a tiny fraction of a second
> - battery sends its electric charge more slowly
> - capacitor produces high energy, but for a short time

Some facts about robots …

- Approximately 30% of robots in the world work on car assembly lines. Around 25% work in electrical or electronics industries.
- About 74% of industrial robots in the world are in the USA, China, Japan, Germany and Korea.
- The Mars robot *Opportunity*, covered over 44 km over the surface of Mars for more than 14 years. The designers planned it to last for only 90 days.
- More than 2.4 million industrial robots are now in use in factories around the world.
- There are about 100 robots for every 10,000 workers in manufacturing industries.

WANTED

Experienced ELECTRONICS ENGINEER at Summit Elektronika

Main Duties: Responsible for a digital audio studio upgrading project. You will supervise a team of senior and junior audio technicians and maintenance staff.

Qualifications Required: a degree in electronics or audio technology

Experience Required: At least five years' experience of audio project management

Send your CV to: Summit Elektronika, PO Box 22, Berlin 10117.

Television satellites are all in orbit about 22,200 miles (35,700 km) above the Earth and travel at approximately 7000 mph (11,000 km/h). At this speed and altitude, the satellite revolves around the planet once every 24 hours, the same period of time it takes the Earth to make one full rotation. In other words, the satellite appears to be permanently at the same location. You therefore only need to direct your dish at the satellite once and then it picks up the signal without further adjustment. Satellites transmit signals in the frequency range of 10.7–12.75 GHz (in Europe). The low noise block (LNB) on the satellite dish on your roof converts this high-frequency signal into a lower signal in the range of 950–2150 MHz.

A GUIDE TO JOB INTERVIEWS PART 3: AT THE INTERVIEW, DON'T …

- dress untidily
- be late for the interview
- be rude or impolite
- talk negatively about your previous employer
- answer only *Yes* or *No*

A GUIDE TO JOB INTERVIEWS PART 2: AT THE INTERVIEW, DO …

- answer every question fully
- be positive and honest about yourself
- ask questions about the job
- show your knowledge about the company
- show you are interested in the job
- talk about your ambitions

TEST RESULTS	ENGINE				
	A	B	C	D	E
0–40 km/h (seconds)	11.48	13.19	9.38	11.74	13.25
Top speed (mph)	44.1	44.4	48.0	46.8	45.0
Sound level (dB)	118	106	121	114	108
Fuel consumption (gph)	3.6	4.1	4.5	7.5	4.0

WANTED

Experienced AUDIO TECHNICIAN at Tower Recording Studios

Main Duties: Maintain and repair digital audio equipment, calculate cost of purchasing new equipment, when required, install new equipment.

Qualifications Required: a diploma in audio technology or electronics

Experience Required: At least two years' experience of audio repair and maintenance

Send your CV to: Tower Music Ltd, PO Box 302, London WC1 2AA.

In 1940, the Tacoma Narrows Bridge in the USA was the third longest suspension bridge in the world with the longest single span in the USA. On 7 November 1940, the wind blew at about 70 km per hour. The deck started moving up and down, and then from side to side. Soon the deck twisted to an angle of 45 degrees, with the result that one side of the deck was 8.5 metres higher than the other side. Next, some suspenders snapped off and a section of the bridge deck broke off from the rest of the bridge and fell into the water below. Immediately, the main cable over that part of the bridge, freed of its weight, tightened like a bow string, flinging suspenders into the air like fishing lines. Then, the whole of the middle section of the bridge collapsed into the water.

Afterwards, engineers tried to discover what caused the collapse. There are four main factors in bridge design: forces, materials, loads and shapes. All these factors caused the collapse of the Tacoma bridge. The wind caused a changing load on the bridge. The flat vertical face of the girder of the bridge deck created resistance to this load. This then produced a torsion (or twisting) force on the deck. The torsion was too powerful for the materials, which were not strong enough to withstand this force.

TEST RESULTS	ENGINE				
	A	B	C	D	E
Shaft length	25 in	20 in	20 in	20 in	25 in
Engine weight	349 lb	496 lb	442 lb	370 lb	407 lb
Power	115 hp @5500 rpm				
Price	$10,000	$10,520	$9490	$8934	$9150

How it works. As a wave moves over the top of the conversion unit, it depresses a disc and the force is transmitted to reciprocating pumps which deliver water to the land. The high-pressure seawater comes ashore in a narrow pipe either (1) to a turbine which produces electricity or (2) to a reverse osmosis filter which produces fresh water.

Advantages. The first benefit is that this system uses waves and wave power, which can be found all over the world. Second, this system has a double function: it can produce electricity (via a turbine) and fresh water (using a reverse osmosis filter). Third, the energy is clean and does not use fossil fuels. Fourth, the converter sits on the sea bed, where it is invisible and safe from storms. Finally, the system does not need a large pipe system. It requires only a small diameter pipe to carry high-pressure seawater ashore.

WANTED

Experienced AUDIO-VISUAL TECHNICIAN at Bond Film Studios

Main Duties: Maintain and repair film cameras and audio-visual equipment, purchase and install new equipment

Qualifications Required: a technician's diploma in film technology

Experience Required: At least two years' experience of working in a film studio

Send your CV to: Bond Studios, PO Box 811, Glasgow G2 5NP.

A GUIDE TO JOB INTERVIEWS PART 1: BEFORE THE INTERVIEW, DO

- find out about the company and the job
- read the job advert carefully and think how your CV matches what they want
- prepare a list of the questions you think the interviewer will ask you
- prepare a list of questions you would like to ask the interviewer

Audio script

Unit 1 Action

🔊 1.1

- **A:** OK, the first thing you've gotta do is bring the new wheel right up to the car. OK?
- **B:** Yeah. I'll get it now.
- **A:** Good. Now, the air pressure in the tyre is probably wrong, so you need to adjust it. OK? Check the pressure, then either let some air out or pump some more air in.
- **B:** Got it. Right, I've done it.
- **A:** Good. Now, before you start lifting up the car, you must loosen the wheel nuts a bit, so get your wheel gun and loosen the nuts. … Done that?
- **B:** Yeah, done it.
- **A:** Right, now you're going to use the jack, so, first of all, put the jack under the front of the car. OK?
- **B:** Yeah.
- **A:** And then raise the front of the car carefully. Have you done that?
- **B:** Yeah.
- **A:** Right, so now take the wheel off and put it down next to you on the ground.
- **B:** Yeah. I've done that.
- **A:** Good. Now, get the new wheel, pick it up and put it on the car. Have you done that?
- **B:** Yes.
- **A:** Right. Now, pick up your wheel gun again and tighten up the wheel nuts.
- **B:** Aha. That's done.
- **A:** Good. Now, lower the car … and … take the jack away.
- **B:** Done it.
- **A:** And, of course, finish off by taking the old wheel away. Just roll it away and put it over there.
- **B:** OK.

🔊 1.2

1. Bring out the new tyres.
2. Lift up the front of the car.
3. Take off the two wheels.
4. Put on the new wheels.
5. Take away the old wheels.
6. Lower the front of the car.
7. Switch off all the electrical systems.
8. Turn on the emergency power source.

Unit 2 Work

🔊 2.1

[T = Tore; K = Ken]

- **T:** Hi, Ken. How are things on your rig?
- **K:** Hi, Tore. Well, we're working very hard at the moment. But I'm going on leave tomorrow.
- **T:** That's great. Where are you going? Back home?
- **K:** I usually go home to Nigeria. But this time I'm flying to France for a holiday.
- **T:** Ah, fantastic. Do you work two weeks on, two weeks off?
- **K:** No, I do three on and three off. How about you?
- **T:** I work two two.
- **K:** When's your next leave?
- **T:** I'm on the helicopter right now! I'm flying to Norway!

🔊 2.2

1. Hi, my name's Billie, and I work in the Sub-Sea crew. I'm an Assistant Sub-Sea Engineer. Basically, I repair and maintain the platform and the pipes under the sea. I report to Mike, the Sub-Sea Engineer.
2. Good morning. My name is Tore, and I'm from Norway. My job title is Assistant Crane Operator. I operate and maintain the cranes on the main deck. I report to the Crane Operator.
3. Hello, I'm Ken. I'm an Assistant Driller, and I operate the drilling equipment. I supervise the Derrickhand and the Pumphand. I report to the Driller. He's the boss.
4. Hi, my name's Adelle and I'm the Chief Electrician on the rig. I maintain and repair all the electrical equipment on the rig. I supervise a team of three Electricians, and I report to the Maintenance Supervisor.

🔊 2.3

[T = Tore; B = Ben]

- **T:** Hello, Deck Crew. Tore speaking.
- **B:** Oh, hi Tore. This is Ben. How's it going?
- **T:** Not bad. But this strong wind is a problem for the cranes. Anyway, what can I do for you?
- **B:** I want to hold a meeting for the deck crew sometime soon.
- **T:** OK. What's the meeting going to be about?
- **B:** I'm going to tell them about the new safety rules for crane operators.
- **T:** OK, that's fine. When are you having the meeting?
- **B:** How about three o'clock next Thursday?
- **T:** Yeah, that's great. Three o'clock next Thursday. See you then. Bye.
- **B:** Cheers. Bye.

🔊 2.4

From 2017 until 2019, I worked at Comet Electronics as a technician. I left Comet in 2019 and became a full-time student at Thames Valley University in September 2019. From 2019 to 2020, I studied audio electronics at Thames Valley. In 2020, I received my Diploma in Audio Technology. Then, in September 2020, I started work as an audio maintenance technician at Omega Studios.

🔊 2.5

1	engineer engine engineering
2	electrician electricity electrical
3	electronics electron electronic
4	mechanic mechanism mechanics mechanical
5	technician technical
6	technologist technology

Unit 3 Comparison

🔊 3.1

[S = Salesperson; C = Customer]

S: How wide is your car?
C: It's just under 1.9 metres wide.
S: OK, that's fine. The vehicle must not be wider than 2 metres.
C: Great.
S: How long is it?
C: It's exactly 7 metres long.
S: Please measure it again carefully. It must not be longer than 7 metres.
C: OK, I'll do that and get back to you.
S: How high is it?
C: It's just over 3.2 metres high, including the bicycles.
S: Mm. That's too high. The vehicle must not be higher than 2.9 metres.
C: OK, I'll take the bikes off.

🔊 3.2

Phone call 1

[J = Julia; MW = Mr Willard]

J: Delta Electronics. This is Customer Service, Julia speaking. How can I help you?
MW: Oh, hello. Do you sell ePhones?
J: Yes, we do. Would you like a pricelist?
MW: Yes, I would. Thanks.
J: Fine. I'll send you one right away. What's your name?
MW: Willard.
J: Sorry, could you repeat that, please?
MW: Willard.
J: How do you spell that?
MW: W-I-L-L-A-R-D.
J: OK. I'll just need a few more details …

Phone call 2

[J = Julia; MJ = Ms Jensen]

J: Delta Electronics. This is Customer Service, Julia speaking. How can I help you?
MJ: Hello. I'd like to order an ePhone, please.
J: Certainly. Which model would you like to order?
MJ: The classic one, please.
J: Fine. Could I have your name, please?
MJ: Jensen.
J: Did you say Johnson?
MJ: No, Jensen. J-E-N-S-E-N.
J: And could you give me your phone number, please?
MJ: 0288 34500

Phone call 3

[J = Julia; MF = Mr Franklin]

J: Delta Electronics. This is Customer Service, Julia speaking. How can I help you?
MF: Hello. I'd like to cancel an order, please.
J: I see. Do you think you could tell me the model number, please?
MF: It was a classic ePhone. I ordered it by phone yesterday.
J: Right. So, do you want me to cancel it?
MF: Yes, please.
J: OK. And what's your name, please?
MF: It's Franklin.
J: Could you repeat that, please?
MF: Franklin.
J: Thank you. And your first name, please?
MF: It's Ken.

Phone call 4

[J = Julia; MM = Ms Martinez]

J: Delta Electronics. This is Customer Service, Julia speaking. How can I help you?
MM: Er, hello. I'd like some information about the ePhone, please.
J: Certainly. What would you like to know?
MM: Well, first of all, what's the screen size?
J: Let's see. Yes, it's 6.2 inches.
MM: Oh, right. It's quite large.
J: Yes. Would you like me to send you the specifications?
MM: Yes, I would. Thanks.
J: Could I have your name, please?
MM: Yes, my name is Martinez.
J: Sorry, did you say Martins?
MM: No, Martinez.
J: And could I have your email address, please?
MM: Yes, it's t.martinez@greenery.co.uk.

Phone call 5

[J = Julia; MB = Mr Brandt]

J: Delta Electronics. This is Customer Service, Julia speaking. How can I help you?
MB: Oh, hello. Yes, I bought a classic ePhone last week, and it doesn't work.
J: Oh, I'm sorry to hear that. What is the problem, exactly?
MB: I can't hear any sound.
J: Right. Shall I put you through to the service department?
MB: Yes, please.
J: OK, hold on. Could you give me your name, please?
MB: It's Brandt.
J: Could you say that again, please?
MB: Brandt.
J: Thanks. I'll transfer you now.

Phone call 6

[J = Julia; MG = Ms Gray]

J: Delta Electronics. This is Customer Service, Julia speaking. How can I help you?
MG: Good morning. I wish to complain about a phone I bought from you.
J: Certainly. Would you mind telling me what the problem is?
MG: The phone doesn't work. I can't make any phone calls.

J: I'm sorry to hear that. Could you give me your name, please?
MG: Yes, my name is Gray.
J: Is that AY or EY?
MG: It's G-R-A-Y.
J: And do you know the order number for your phone, please?
B: Yes, it's 3022.

🔊 3.3

A: Hello, I'd like to buy a DAB radio, please.
B: Certainly. We have two colours, red or black. And there are two models. There's one with Bluetooth streaming, and there's one without Bluetooth. Which one would you like?
A: I'd like the red one with Bluetooth, please.

Unit 4 Processes

🔊 4.1

This monster is one of the largest hard-rock tunnel boring machines, or TBMs, ever made for the USA. It's the Robbins Main Beam TBM, also called Big Tex, and its job is to drill a 7.8-kilometre tunnel to protect the city of Dallas in Texas from flood water. Big Tex is over 70 metres long, and its cutter head is 11.6 metres in diameter at the beginning of the tunnel. Then, under halfway through, a narrower tunnel is needed, so the diameter of the cutter head changes to 9.9 metres. This makes it probably the world's first variable-diameter TBM. Project managers expect that the TBM will move forward through the rock at a speed of about 25 metres per day.

Unit 5 Descriptions

🔊 5.1

a) **A:** So, tell me about this invention. What's it for?
   B: It's for finding lost items.
b) **A:** OK. And what about this device. What's it used for?
   B: It's used for charging an electric vehicle on the roadside without a charging station.
c) **A:** Tell me about this invention. What can it be used for?
   B: You can use it to move quickly over and under water.

🔊 5.2

1 triangle
2 rectangular
3 circular
4 cylinder
5 triangular
6 circle
7 rectangle
8 cylindrical

🔊 5.3

1 **A:** So, tell me about this invention. What does it do?
   B: This invention is an electronic device which can boil eggs without using water.
2 **A:** So, tell me about this invention. What is it? What's it for?
   B: LifeGuard is an alarm system that can find someone who has fallen off a boat.

3 **A:** So, let's hear about this invention. What is it and what's its purpose?
   B: This is a do-it yourself kit which enables you to repair your smartphone if it has fallen into some water.
4 **A:** So, why don't you tell me about this invention. What exactly is it for?
   B: It's a seat-belt adjuster that protects children in car booster seats.

Unit 6 Procedures

🔊 6.1

A: Right, let's brainstorm for a moment. Your diving partner is trapped under water. What do you need to do? Just come up with ideas, quickly, in any order.
B: Get their leg free from the wreckage, or rocks, or whatever.
C: We've gotta bring them up from the bottom of the sea to the surface.
D: You gotta get them OUT of the water.
A: Mm. Right, good. Any other ideas?
B: Well, you have to find them first. You need to locate them.
D: Yeah, you find them and then you've got to mark their position. Use a buoy on the surface.
C: You should give them extra oxygen, more gas, if their own oxygen is low.
A: Good, you're doing well. What else do you need to do?
D: Give them artificial respiration, if they're not breathing.
C: When they're on the surface of the sea, you have to make them float, make them buoyant.
B: When they're on the surface, you need to tow them to safety, you know, pull them to a boat or something.
A: Yeah, this is good stuff. Anything else?
B: You may have to attract help at the surface. Shout or shine a light to other boats.
C: Take them to hospital.
D: Yeah, but give them first aid, if they need it.
A: Great. OK. Let's look at these ideas again.

🔊 6.2

A: OK, now let's look at all the ideas in this spidergram, and put them in the best order, the best sequence of events. So, let's start at the beginning. What if we don't know exactly where the diver is? If their location underwater is unknown? What should we do first?
B: We have to locate the diver, and then mark their position with a buoy on the surface.
C: And then we can cut them free, with a knife, if they're trapped.
A: Right, and what about their oxygen supply?
D: If their breathing gas is low, we have to give them some more gas. We can use an extra oxygen tank.
B: And then we should bring them up to the surface, very carefully and not too quickly.
A: Right, good, so you're at the surface, and you're holding the diver there. What if they sink again?
C: We need to make them float, make them buoyant at the surface. We can inflate their jacket.
D: If they're not breathing, we may have to give them artificial respiration there on the surface.

B: And call for help, if there are any other boats around. Or send a signal for help.
A: What if there's no help available? You're on the surface, but there are no other boats around?
B: Tow them to the boat, or to the land if it's close.
C: Then remove them from the water and get them into the boat or onto land.
D: If they need immediate treatment, give them first aid.
B: And if the injury is serious, call a helicopter to take them to hospital.
A: Good, well done.

🔊 6.3

1

[C1 = Caller 1; R = Receptionist]

C1: Oh, hello, erm, do you think you could tell me how to get to the Engineering Department in the university?
R: Of course. Where are you at the moment?
C1: I'm driving up the M95 motorway from the south.
R: OK. Well, you have to leave the motorway at Junction 3. You'll see the sign.
C1: Right. So I leave the M95 at Junction 3?
R: Yeah. Then, when you come off the slip road of the motorway, you'll come to a large roundabout.
C1: OK.
R: Take the … uh … how many? … um, the fifth exit. Yes, the fifth exit from the roundabout. One of the exits is no entry because it's a slip road from the motorway.
C1: OK. Fifth exit.
R: Then, almost immediately, you'll come to the main entrance to the South Campus.
C1: Right.
R: So then, turn left into the campus and go straight ahead.
C1: OK.
R: You'll see four buildings on your left.
C1: Four buildings on my left.
R: Yes. And the Engineering Department is the last building on your left.
C1: Great. Thanks very much.
R: You're welcome.

2

[C2 = Caller 2; R = Receptionist]

C2: Hi, yeah, er, could you please tell me how to get to the Sports Centre in the university?
R: Sure. Where are you now?
C2: I'm coming out of the entrance to the South Campus.
R: Are you driving a car?
C2: Yes, I am.
R: OK … well, erm, come out of the entrance and turn right at the T-junction.
C2: OK.
R: Soon you'll come to a large roundabout over the M95 motorway.
C2: Right …
R: Go round the roundabout, pass the no-entry slip road, and take the second main exit. You're in Comet Way. Keep going until you come to the next roundabout.
C2: OK.
R: So, turn left at this roundabout. It's the first exit. Soon you'll come to another small roundabout. There's a hotel on your left at the roundabout.
C2: OK.
R: At this roundabout, take the second exit.
C2: OK.
R: There's another roundabout ahead of you. Go straight ahead at this roundabout, second exit. Now you're going past the main entrance of the North Campus.
C2: Yeah.
R: At the next roundabout, turn left. Follow the road around to the left. You'll see the North Campus on your left.
C2: OK.
R: Just before you come to the next crossroads, you'll see a large building on your left.
C2: OK. A large building on my left. Just before the crossroads.
R: That's right. That building is the Sports Centre.
C2: Thanks. Got it!

Unit 7 Services

🔊 7.1

[L = Lisa; C1 = Caller 1]

1

L: Technical support. Lisa here. What's up?
C1: Hi, Lisa. I can't log into the network. It says **WRONG PASSWORD**.
L: Right. Are you sure that you're typing the correct password.
C1: The password appears automatically.
L: Oh, right. You must have checked the **REMEMBER PASSWORD** box.
C1: Ah, yes, I have. So, what do I do?
L: Uncheck the box, OK?
C1: Yes.
L: Now try typing in the correct password.
C1: Right. Yes, I've done it. I've logged in. Thanks, Lisa.

2

[L = Lisa; C2 = Caller 2]

L: Technical support. Lisa here.
C2: Oh hi, Lisa. It's Rod.
L: You again! So, what's wrong now?
C2: Hi, Lisa. Yeah, sorry, it's me. Well, this time my monitor isn't working. I can't see the whole page. I can only see part of the page.
L: Aha. And are the icons and words too big?
C2: Yep. That's right.
L: OK. Well, your computer must be using the wrong screen resolution settings.
C2: Oh, right. So, what should I do?
L: You should go to *Control panel*. Click on *Display*, then *Settings*.
C2: Right, I've done that …
L: Then you should move the slider up. Increase the screen resolution.
C2: OK, done it.

3

[L = Lisa; C3 = Caller 3]

Audio script 123

L: Technical support. Lisa here. What's the problem?
C3: Hi, Lisa. Well, I can't open any email attachments.
L: OK. How about the emails themselves? Can you open them all right?
C3: Yes, the emails are fine. But when I double-click on the attachments, nothing happens.
L: Well, your email program may be blocking the attachments.
C3: Oh, right. So, what can I do?
L: Open *Tools – Options – Security*. Try lowering your security level.
C3: OK. I'll try that. Thanks.

4

[L = Lisa; C4 = Caller 4]

L: Technical support. Lisa here. How can I help?
C4: Hi, Lisa. I'm using the Internet. When I click on a link, nothing happens.
L: OK. Is it a pop-up?
C4: I don't know. It says **CLICK HERE TO SEE PHOTO.** But, when I click, I don't see the photo.
L: It may be a pop-up. Do you have a firewall?
C4: Yes.
L: OK, your firewall might be blocking the pop-ups.
C4: Right. So, what should I do now?
L: I suggest you try unblocking the pop-ups. Open your firewall program.
C4: OK, I've done that.
L: Does it say *block pop-up adverts*?
C4: Yes.
L: Try unchecking the box. Then clear your cache, refresh your web page and try again.
C4: OK, I'll try that. Thanks, Lisa.

5

[L = Lisa; C5 = Caller 5]

L: Technical support. Lisa here. What's the problem?
C5: Hi, Lisa. Yeah. Bill here. I've set up a wireless router in the next room to my computer. But I can't get a connection between the router and the computer.
L: Aha. How far is the router from the computer?
C5: It's only about eight metres away.
L: Well, another electronic device could be interfering with the connection.
C5: Oh, right. What kind of device?
L: It could be a cordless phone, a microwave oven, anything really. Do you have a cordless phone?
C5: Yes, I do.
L: It must be that.
C5: So, what should I do?
L: Well, you could move the phone away. Or why don't you move the router around? I suggest you try moving the router to a different location. Then try the connection again.
C5: OK, I'll try moving the router. Thanks, Lisa.

6

[L = Lisa; C6 = Caller 6]

L: Technical support. Lisa here. What's up?
C6: Hi, Lisa. It's Bill again.
L: Aha, hello, Bill. Is it your wireless connection?
C6: Yes. I've connected my computer to the router. Thanks.
L: Good.
C6: But I can't access the Internet.
L: Is there a message on the screen?
C6: Yes. It says **LITTLE OR NO CONNECTIVITY**.
L: Aha. Well, it must be an IP problem. You must have given the computer a different IP address from the router.
C6: Right. So, how can I fix that?
L: Why don't you try rebooting the router first? If that doesn't work, try rebooting the computer and then the router again.
C6: OK, I'll do that. Thanks.

🔊 **7.2**

1 You must have checked the **REMEMBER PASSWORD** box.
2 Your computer must be using the wrong screen resolution settings.
3 Your email program may be blocking the attachments.
4 Your firewall might be blocking the pop-ups.
5 Another electronic device could be interfering with the connection.
6 You must have given the computer a different IP address from the router.

🔊 **7.3**

1 Now try typing in the correct password.
2 Try lowering your security level.
3 Well, you could move the phone away. Or why don't you move the router around?
4 I suggest you try moving the router to a different location.

🔊 **7.4**

[S = Steve; C = Customer]

S: Good morning, customer service. My name is Steve. How can I help you?
C: Yes, good morning. I wish to complain about a printer I bought from you.
S: Oh, I'm sorry to hear that. What exactly is the problem?
C: The AC adapter with the printer doesn't work.
S: I see. Did it work the first time you switched it on?
C: No, it didn't.
S: Well, I do apologise for that. It must be our fault. What model of printer is it?
C: It's a 3845.
S: And could I have your name, please?
C: Yes, my name is Maria Beck.
S: … And do you have your receipt there?
C: Yes.
S: That's great. Could you read out the order number, please? It's at the top on the right.
C: Errm. Yes, order number … it's 89054.
S: Great. … Right, Ms Beck. Let me just summarise the situation. You've told me that the adapter with your 3845 printer doesn't work and has never worked. Is that correct?
C: Correct.
S: Well, I'm pleased to tell you that we will replace your adapter and the printer. You will receive the goods by the end of the week. We have your address. We'll collect the old printer at the same time.
C: Great.

S: And I'm happy to say that we're going to give you five euros discount off your next purchase.
C: That's very reasonable. Thank you.
S: You're welcome, Ms Beck. Have a nice day.

Unit 8 Energy

🔊 8.1

Good morning, everyone. Today, I'm going to talk about the Wave Energy Converter.
You're probably wondering what a Wave Energy Converter is. So, let's have a simple definition to start with. Very simply, a Wave Energy Converter is a system which converts the energy from sea waves into electrical power.
Before I talk about the system itself, let me tell you where it is located, because some systems are located on the surface of the sea, and some on the seashore. But not this system. The Wave Energy Converter is fixed to the sea bed.
OK, now let's look at the main components. The Wave Energy Converter has five main components or parts. These are: a very large flexible disc, a lever, a chamber which takes in seawater, a set of pistons, many seawater pipes, and of course a turbine on the land.
The main specifications of the system are as follows. The whole system on the sea bed is 4.6 metres high and 20.4 metres long; the main pipe is 125 millimetres wide; the pressure of the water in the pipes is 7000 kilopascals, or 1000 psi, that's pounds per square inch. The complete system can generate 100 kilowatts of electricity.
OK, that's enough number-crunching. Let's look at how the system works. Here's a very simple account of the operation of the system. Let's start with the sea. The sea wave oscillates. This oscillating motion pushes the disc down in a linear motion. The disc makes the lever oscillate. The oscillating lever makes the pistons move in a reciprocating motion. Then the pistons push seawater from the chamber through the pipe at high pressure. The high-pressure water then makes the turbine rotate. This generates electricity.
So, that's how it works. This system has great benefits. The most important benefit is that wave energy is a renewable energy resource; and, of course, it uses no fossil fuels.

Unit 10 Forces

🔊 10.1

1	tensile	tension
2	compressive	compression
3	rigid	rigidity
4	flexibility	flexible
5	elasticity	elastic
6	plastic	plasticity

🔊 10.2

Good afternoon, everyone, and welcome. The aim of my talk today is to discuss the problem of earthquakes and the damage they cause to buildings, and some solutions to this problem. I'd like to begin by talking about what causes earthquakes. As you know, the tectonic plates on the Earth's surface, have been moving for millions of years, and they're still moving. Sometimes, this movement causes the surface to break. This break or fracture in the Earth's crust is called a fault. When the rock breaks, there is a sudden release of energy. Shock waves spread out through and around the Earth in all directions, starting from the focus, or epicentre, of the earthquake. At the Earth's surface, the ground vibrates as the waves pass through it. This is what we call an earthquake.
And that brings me to the problem which earthquakes cause for buildings. The problem for buildings is that, during an earthquake, the ground moves in all directions. It moves horizontally. It moves up and down. It rotates and it twists. All these movements affect buildings. But horizontal movement is the most damaging for a building. As you can see in the photograph, if a building moves too much from side to side the structure can collapse.
So, now let's move on to talk about some solutions to this problem.

🔊 10.3

So, now let's move on to talk about some solutions to this problem. There are several methods you can use to make a building earthquake-resistant. I will mention only three of these. Very briefly, the first method I'll describe is to make a building stronger, for example, by using diagonal braces, as you can see in Slide 1.
Then, I'll go on to the second method, which, very briefly, is to make the structure more flexible, by adding a damper to the brace, as shown in Slide 2.
Then, finally, I'll move on to talk about the third method, shown in Slide 3, which is to install a large heavy weight near the top of the building, to cancel out the force of the earthquake.
So, now let's look at these three methods in more detail …

Unit 11 Design

🔊 11.1

1
[I = Interviewer; P1 = Participant]

I: Good morning. Welcome to the Industrial Robot Convention. I hope you're enjoying it. I'm doing a survey to find out how people use robots and what improvements can be made. Would you mind if I ask you some questions?
P1: Sure, go ahead.
I: First of all, would you mind telling me what you do and where you work?
P1: Yes, I'm a construction engineer, and I specialise in building work on high-rise buildings and skyscrapers.
I: I see you are looking at the SnakeBot. Do you use one in your work?
P1: Yes, but I use an older model.
I: What do you think of it? Does it help your work?
P1: Yes, if I forget to take a tool to the top of a building, I tap an instruction on my tablet and the SnakeBot brings it to me.
I: So, what are the advantages of the SnakeBot?

P1: Well, its main strength is that it can twist around things such as girders, pipes and scaffolding. In addition, it is strong enough to carry small loads such as spanners and hammers, and bring them up to me at the top of a building.
I: Excellent. So, would you say that it has any drawbacks or disadvantages?
P1: Yes, its main weakness is that, although the SnakeBot can navigate autonomously, I still have to give it commands from my tablet. It's a bit time-consuming, because I can't do my building work and tap out instructions at the same time.
I: So, in the future, how would you suggest that it could be improved?
P1: Well, it would be great if the designers could add voice activation to the model.

2

[I = Interviewer; P2 = Participant 2]

I: Hello. Welcome to the Industrial Robot Convention. I'm doing a survey to find out how people use robots and what improvements can be made. Would you mind if I ask you some questions?
P2: I'm a bit busy. Oh, all right, go on, ask away.
I: Thanks. Well, first of all, what do you do and where do you work?
P2: I'm an emergency first responder. I search for people and try to rescue them from under collapsed buildings, after a major disaster, such as an earthquake or explosion.
I: And which robot do you use in your work?
P2: I use a Rescue Robot.
I: What do you think of it? Does the Rescue Robot help your work?
P2: Yes, it helps me to locate people buried under collapsed buildings.
I: So, what would you say are its main strengths?
P2: Well, I would say it has two important advantages. First of all, it can access areas which are potentially dangerous for humans to go into. It can easily move over and under things, and it can get into spaces which are too small for me to climb into. In addition to this, its camera and microphone are more sensitive than human eyes and ears.
I: So, do you think it has any drawbacks or weaknesses?
P2: Well, one thing I've noticed is that the robot I use is too big and heavy to climb over very large piles of rubble.
I: So, looking into the future, how do you suggest we could modify or improve it?
P2: Well, it's very simple really. You just need to keep making smaller, lighter versions of it. The latest model looks really lightweight, so that's good.
I: I see. Well, thanks very much indeed for sparing me your time.
P2: Don't mention it.

🔊 11.2

[I = Interviewer; P1 = Participant 1]

I: So, what are the advantages of the SnakeBot?
P1: Well, its main strength is that it can twist around things like girders, pipes and scaffolding.
I: Excellent. So, would you say that it has any drawbacks, or disadvantages?

P1: Yes, its main weakness is that you have to control every movement with a joystick.
I: So, in the future, how would you suggest that it could be improved?
P1: Well, I would suggest that you should design a voice-activated SnakeBot.

🔊 11.3

Good morning, everyone, and thanks for coming.
The aim of this short presentation is to tell you about our new traction kite for cargo ships and supertankers.
I'd like to start by asking a question. Why do we need a traction kite?
Well, as we all know, cargo ships and supertankers weigh tens of thousands of tons. And the diesel oil that drives these ships is non-renewable and very expensive. We need to use less oil. So, we need to use wind energy. We need to use sails to harness that energy.
So, what is the problem with other designs for sails?
Other designs use a fixed and permanent mast and sail. But this is very expensive for the ship owners, as they need to buy a new boat, or fix a mast and sail to their boats.
And that brings me to our design brief.
Our brief was to design a traction kite which is strong enough to pull a large cargo ship through the water. It must be detachable – that means it can be removed from the ship.
Now, let's move on to materials. What is the traction kite made of? And what are the properties of the materials?
Well, the kite is made of a special polyester. This material is tough but flexible and lightweight. It has very high tensile strength and low friction.
Right, so now let's look at the main parts of the traction kite and their function.
As you can see in the diagram, the kite has two very large sails. These are attached to a large oval balloon. The balloon is filled with helium. A small capsule is suspended from the balloon. This capsule contains a three-man crew and computers. There are sensors on the wings. These sensors detect air pressure and air speed, and send data to the computers. The computers control the speed and direction of the kite. The kite is connected to the client ship using a strong cable.
So, how large is this kite? And how high does it fly? Let's look at some dimensions.
Well, it's a giant kite. The wingspan is 120 metres from wing tip to wing tip. The area of the sail is 5000 square metres. And it flies about 300 metres above sea level.
All right, now let's turn to the operation of the kite. How does it work?
The kite crew steer the kite to a client ship. They drop the cable to the ship and the ship's crew attach the cable to the ship. The kite then catches the wind and pulls the ship along with about 6000 horsepower. When the wind direction changes, or the wind drops, the kite is untied from the ship and travels to another client ship.
And finally, I'd like to mention some of the advantages of the traction kite.
The kite uses wind power, which is a renewable source. Ships which use the traction kite can use 35% less fuel on a voyage.

Carbon emissions are also reduced. And the system is less expensive for the ship owners. They don't have to buy new ships with sails. They simply pay to use the kite sail when they need it.

Unit 12 Innovation

🔊 12.1

[P = Presenter; M = Michela]

P: Hello and welcome to the show. This week, we're looking at new car safety systems, and in the studio we have an expert on car safety, Michela Rossi. Welcome, Michela. So, which car safety system would you like to tell us about first?
M: Hello Jane, and thanks for having me on the programme. Well, I'd like to tell you something about intelligent cruise control systems.
P: Intelligent cruise control? That sounds interesting. What does it do exactly?
M: Well, it's a safety system which maintains a safe distance between your car and the vehicle in front of you.
P: And why do you think drivers need this system?
M: Well, you see, the statistics show that many road accidents are caused when the vehicle in front suddenly stops.
P: So, you believe this invention prevents some of those accidents from happening?
M: Yes, that's right.
P: And what technology or principle is this invention based on?
M: Well, it makes use of laser technology and the principle of radar. And, of course, it uses sensor technology. As well as these technologies, it also makes use of the latest developments in satellite navigation and mapping, as well as cameras to recognise road signs and so on.
P: But, the main component is a laser sensor?
M: That's right. A laser sensor and a computer which is connected to the braking and acceleration systems.
P: Where is the sensor located?
M: The sensor's mounted on the front of the vehicle. It's built into the windscreen, at the top.
P: So, tell me about its operation. How does it work?
M: Well, first of all, you key in the distance you want to maintain between your car and the vehicle in front. So, if it's raining, for instance, you can key in a longer distance. Then the system works automatically. If your car moves too close to the one in front, the sensor activates the brakes. And if your car moves too far behind, the sensor activates the accelerator a little. But you can over-ride the system by touching the brakes or acceleration pedal yourself.
P: That's very interesting. And I suppose the system is becoming more and more intelligent all the time?
M: Yes, that's right. The system can use data from cameras on the car and satnav maps to automate acceleration and braking at highway exits, entrances, junctions and roundabouts, as well as changes in speed limit.

P: So, just to sum up for us, could you tell us very briefly, what are the benefits or advantages of the intelligent cruise control system?
M: Well, I expect it will reduce the chances of a serious accident. It's automatic and it thinks much faster than the driver.
P: Michela Rossi, thank you very much for talking to us.
M: You're welcome.

🔊 12.2

A: Good morning, and welcome to the programme. Today I'm interviewing Michela Rossi, who works for Central Motors. We'll be talking about her, and about her career in automotive technology. Good morning, Michela.
B: Good morning, Jane.
A: And how long have you worked for Central Motors?
B: I've been here for about four years now.
A: I see. So what's your job title? Inventor?
B: No, no. I'm a design engineer. I work in a team of designers and inventors.
A: And how many things have you invented?
B: I think, with the team, I've designed or invented five, no, six new products since I joined Central Motors.
A: That's fantastic. So, what qualifications do you have?
B: I have a technician's diploma from Toulouse Technical Institute and an engineering degree from the Polytechnic University of Turin.
A: Great. So, Michela, let's talk a little about your future intentions. Are you planning to invent anything else in the near future?
B: Yes, I am. In fact, I'll be working on a new type of rear camera for cars. The camera will see obstructions and will warn the driver.
A: I see. And after that, what are your long-term plans for your career?
B: Ah, who knows? I'll continue working here in Central Motors for several years, I hope. Then I may start my own design company.
A: Well, Michela, it's been very interesting talking to you. And good luck with your career.
B: Thanks very much.

Pearson Education Limited
KAO Two
KAO Park
Hockham Way
Harlow, Essex
CM17 9SR
England
and Associated Companies throughout the world.

pearsonenglish.com

© Pearson Education Limited 2022

Written by David Bonamy

The right of David Bonamy to be identified as author of this Work has been asserted by him in accordance with the Copyright, Designs and Patents Act 1988

All rights reserved; no part of this publication may be reproduced, stored in a retrieval system, or transmitted in any form or by any means, electronic, mechanical, photocopying, recording, or otherwise without the prior written permission of the Publishers.

First published 2008
This edition published 2022
Fifth impression 2023

ISBN: 978-1-292-42447-7

Set in Source sans pro-Light
Printed and Bound by Neografia, Slovakia

Acknowledgements
Illustrated by Mark Duffin, Peter Harper, HL Studios and Gowthaman S

Image Credit(s):

123RF: Aaron Bass 70, Cathy Yeulet 17, Jozef Polc 12, kurhan 7, lightfieldstudios 95, liravega258 40, Mark Agnor 11, Olga Yastremska 22, Vampy1 49

Airbus MAVERIC: Airbus 86

Airbus ZEROe: Airbus 86

Alamy: Cavan Images 76, Cultura RM 38, David J. Green - energy 70, Everett Collection Historical 74, Eye Ubiquitous 7, i creative 70, Ian Dagnall 38, imageBROKER 83, Ingram Publishing 35, LatitudeStock 38, Rupert Oberhäuser 90, Science History Images 98, 99, Scott London 65, Visual&Written SL 58

Boeing: Boeing 86

Carnegie Mellon University: Carnegie Mellon University 84

Eelume: Eelume 84

Getty Images: Andy Sotiriou 46, BartCo 49, choness 65, Janine Brauneis 83, Johannes Mann 56, Jon Feingersh 4, kycstudio COV, 1, Lu ShaoJi 8, Lubo Ivanko 37, luoman 65, Paul Burns 14, Tay Jnr 11, TORU YAMANAKA 70

Gozney Roccbox: Gozney Roccbox 112

Joe Doucet: Joe Doucet 86

John MacNeill Illustration: John MacNeill Illustration 26

Kestrel Meters: Kestrel Meters 37

MIRA: Virtual Incision Corporation, MIRA 84

PunchStock: Corbis 10, 11, Simple Stock Shots 70

SCIENCE PHOTO LIBRARY LIMITED: JAMES KING-HOLMES 70, RIA NOVOSTI 66

Shutterstock: 2Ban 8, Aleksandra Berzhets 65, Andrey_Popov 52, designkida 36, Dustie 65, FabrikaSimf 68, Fotosenmeer 70, fotostory 65, 76, freevideophotoagency 24, Goodluz 15, HikoPhotography 76, JonMilnes 11, Kekyalyaynen 9, littlesam 48, manfredxy 49, metamorworks 37, MyImages - Micha 49, NosorogUA 99, Pixel-Shot 8, Robert Kneschke 96, Scharfsinn 99, Shutterstock 17, 38, Vectordidak 8, yosmoes815 99, Yuri Hoyda 8

SparkCharge: SparkCharge 36

Taipei Financial Center Corp.: Taipei Financial Center Corp. 76

Teledyne Flir: Teledyne Flir 84

Cover images: Front: iStockphoto: Kristian Stensoenes

All other images © Pearson Education